Fleeing the Country:

Rural Alaska through the Eyes of a Child

by Eartha Lee

Eartha Lee

First published by Dog Ear Publishing
4010 W. 86th Street, Ste H
Indianapolis, IN 46268
www.dogearpublishing.net

ISBN: 978-145750-764-9

This book is printed on acid-free paper.

Printed in the United States of America

*This story is dedicated
to the children of Alaska.*

*   *   *

I am most fortunate for
my niece and nephew,
my sister and brother,
my mother and father,
and my grandparents.

*   *   *

I wish to personally thank
Michelle McFalls,
Todd Liebross,
and Jim Kenaston
for their enduring
compassion and friendship.

*   *   *

I continue to learn the beauty of truth from Blue Six,
an extraordinary group of people who have shown me that
charity is still very much vibrant and alive.

*   *   *

I offer eternal respect for my Spiritual Creator,
an ever-present force that has mystically guided
me through what is often called time.

*   *   *

I will forever pay tribute to the life of Harold Joseph Day.

*   *   *

TABLE OF CONTENTS

The air is mine, oh precious air,
which makes me all I am.
The wind belongs to me when it blows my way,
and it makes me restless.

PROLOGUE

THE TAYLOR HIGHWAY, graveled and dusty, stretches ahead deep into the wilderness of Alaska towards the Yukon River. Curves have been carved into the mountainsides, creating sharp bends and twists for miles upon end. The road is narrow and scarred with pits worn deep into the surface from water rushing down the steep slopes. Signs warn of falling rocks from above. There are no guardrails.

Higher up, the road evens out as it lazily winds through the tundra, marking the beginning of a new country. Dwarfish shrubs and stunted trees scream upwards, while down below wildflowers spring forth wearing nothing but a fleeting dash of color. The mountains spread out, hill upon hill, a never-ending ripple that runs into the great sky.

We are finally returning, my brother and I. My mind wanders as we pass mile after mile of straggly undergrowth dotted with a few struggling trees. The world here is already beginning to be claimed by the cold shadows of the last autumn of the century. Soon the road will be a blinding fury of snow and wind and drifts, impassable by vehicle from mid-October to mid-April.

I am driving thirty-five miles an hour forward into my past. Here the road becomes more perilous with each passing mile-post. For the last decade, the straggly barren land has remained markedly unchanged. Trees and shrubs that seemed to be dying years ago still look as if they are barely surviving. I roll down the window to taste the pure brisk air outside. A cool wind rushes through the car, and drops of rain softly brush across my cheek.

"There's Gravel Gulch," John Charles says. I slow to a crawl as we look down below at the little cabin still standing in the midst of the woods, and images flash through my mind. For a moment, I climb up the cliffs with my sister again, our legs all scrawny and our hair tangled with twigs. We fall yet bruised legs mean nothing to us. We just pick ourselves up and yell small screams that echo into all that we know.

Several miles ahead, we pass the old American Creek Campground, now buried beneath overgrown raspberry bushes and little new trees. But for me, the sites are still filled with travelers searching for gold in the banks by the creek. Daddy is struck with the fever, dragging John Charles along with dreams of striking it rich. I run through the trails barefoot with Sara, and we look in cracks between rocks for gold of our own. Soon the Taylor Highway becomes Amundsen Street, the main road that runs through the center of Eagle. At the yield sign, I take a right on the road to Eagle Village, three miles upriver.

Both communities have a symbiotic relationship with one another—Eagle (with about 130 residents, a grocery store and a gas station, the post office, a laundromat with public showers, a restaurant, the school, the library, and several museums) and Eagle Village (home to nearly 50 Athabaskan Natives, the clinic, the public safety office, and Charlie's Hall). Yet the city and the village are distinctly and vastly different as they are influenced by differences in ethnicity and heritage. They even function under separate governments. The city has a mayor, city council, and a hired city clerk, while the Natives have a tribal council led by a chief.

A little past the Village Store, on the outskirts of the far side of Eagle, I turn onto a dead end lane, parking in front of a cabin with a treasure of junk in the yard. As we get out of the car, dogs bark in the background, begging to be set free from their chains. John Charles walks with me to the front door, and I give it several strong knocks.

The door opens, and there is my father in front of me. "Well, well, look who's here." He gives me that twisted sideways grin that I know so well, and a sad sparkle twinkles in his eyes when I catch his gaze. Do I hug or no?—and then I have my arm halfway around his thinned body. The smell of tobacco fills the room, a familiar scent of home.

CHAPTER ONE

"She Ain't Leavin'"

"SHE MIGHT THINK she's leavin', but she ain't," Al said as he took a sip of coffee.

"She's already packed up her stuff, hasn't she?" The waitress asked. She headed towards him with a coffee pot ready in hand.

"That don't make a difference, she ain't leavin'." He pushed his cup over to the edge of the table. "She ain't. It's that simple. Not if I don't let her. Her mama seems to act like it'd be a good idea—her goin' away to the bright lights and big cities and all—but it's the last thing that girl needs. When she turns eighteen, she can do what she wants, but like it sez in the Bible, 'children obey your parents', and I'll be derned if she's gonna tell me what's gonna happen in this family. Ever since she started up at that public school, she's just got on a high horse that she's gonna do whatever she feels like."

The waitress poured him yet another cup of coffee. "From the way she's been talking, she's already made up her mind."

"I done tole you, she ain't leavin'."

Outside in front of the restaurant, a crowd of tourists milled about Front Street. Many carried cameras, snapping shot after shot of the view of the Yukon. Others gazed off into the distance. The river disappeared behind Eagle Bluff, a steep cliff with three peaks that climbed high into the sky. In the middle

1

of the river, Belle Isle barely reached above the surface of the water, just a little beach sprinkled with a forest of trees.

Every morning the Yukon Queen brought the tourists in from Dawson City. Soon after crossing the Canadian border, the Yukon Queen reached the boat dock of Eagle, and everyone stepped off to finally stand upon the Great Land of the Last Frontier. The typical package deal included the cost of the cruise down the river and transportation out of Eagle by bus on the Taylor.

The city of Eagle—fertile with a rich history from the Gold Rush days—offered a tour for a small fee to those who wanted to see the museums. The tour started at the Customs House Museum and then went on to the old Wickersham Courthouse. A local guide pointed out well-preserved remnants from the past as they walked through the buildings, describing in detail the role that many of them played as the town had developed over the decades. After a short stroll up the grassy airfield that was once the old military parade ground, the group continued with an excursion through the Mule Barn, an exceptionally long narrow building lined with antiquated relics on both sides.

At mid-day, the Gray Line bus waited with its engine running nearby the restaurant. It would soon be time to board. After the bus departed, a few kids bicycled and wandered out into the now quiet street. The side door to the restaurant slammed behind Al, and as he walked towards the '57 Chevy, he hoisted up his jeans with one hand while putting on his wide-brimmed leather hat with the other.

CHAPTER TWO

"Crossing the Border"

AS SOON AS I turned fourteen, I could get an official job. Until then, there were plenty of ways to earn money without having to fill out official paperwork. I babysat, fish-sat, cat-sat, dog-sat, and picked berries to sell to my faithful customers.

Once I was old enough to pay taxes, I started working for the city under the auspices of the Alaska Youth Grant Program. Minimum wage was quite a raise from what I'd been earning before, and I could almost always get forty hours a week. I helped paint the Well House a new coat of white, took minutes at city council meetings, read stories to little kids in the library, and hauled rocks to build a wall around the old Customs House Museum.

John Charles was in Alaska for the season working with a new friend he had made on the job in a fishery down in the Kenai Peninsula. He planned to come up to Eagle for a visit before his fall classes started back at Middle Tennessee State University. His friend, Jamie, needed a ride to the bus station in Edmonton. Jamie had decided that joining John Charles would be better than trying to hitchhike the Alcan. In early August, John Charles drove into Eagle in his trusty Toyota truck with his dog Bogart and Jamie.

I was desperate to go back South with my brother. Grandma and Grandpa had told me months earlier that I was welcome to live with them and finish high school in Blairsville.

John Charles told Mom, "If it's okay with you, I'll give Eartha a ride back to Georgia. I don't care what Al says. I'll take her if you don't have any objections."

Even though Dad liked to say otherwise, Mom had taught me that I was my own human being, and she was going to let me make my own choices. "I'm not going to stand in her way. My mama ruled my life for way too long, and I don't want to make the same mistake with Eartha. I think she's old enough to decide for herself." The next day, I finished packing my boxes. I knew what I had to do. Get out of Eagle.

Dad was furious—he believed that I was his property until I turned the magical age of eighteen—but he didn't dare lay a hand on me with so many eyes on him. If he even so much as tried, I could end up being medivacked out to the Fairbanks Hospital, and the troopers would be called in to investigate what had happened.

He wasn't going to keep quiet about it though. "You ain't goin', so you might as well get the idea out of your head. I done tole you. I don't care what your mama says or anybody else. Once you're eighteen, you can—" I was done listening. He might as well get the idea out of *his* head. I was leaving. And that was that.

"I don't care what you say, Dad. The only way you're gonna keep me here is tie me up and put me in the root cellar. Are you going to tie me up and put me in the root cellar?" I glared at him with brown eyes that matched his own.

He fought to find one last weapon that wouldn't involve the law being called in to check out any visible child abuse. "Well—if y'all are gonna leave, you ain't stickin' around for any more visitin'." Dad looked at John Charles with violence raging in his eyes like a storm in the middle of an especially harsh winter. "You get on the road tomorrow. First thing."

We awoke early in the morning, and John Charles helped me load up my boxes. Dad started in with his diatribe again. "That's it! You get in that truck, and you won't be my daughter anymore. That's it. You get in that truck, and I'll disown you. I mean it. I'm tellin' you, I'll disown you!"

"I don't care if you disown me! You never owned me in the first place!" I hollered back at him. "And I am leaving! You can't stop me!" There was no way he was going to even begin to look for a rope. He knew better if he didn't want to end up in jail or a mental hospital.

While John Charles made sure that Bogart was settled in for the ride, I walked across the road to say goodbye to Phil. He didn't answer the door after several knocks, so I opened the door to see if he was still sleeping, but he was not at home. Suddenly screams rose up inside of me, "You don't want to leave, you don't want to leave, you have to find Phil. You *have* to find Phil . . . !"

I got on my bicycle right away and rode all around town, mud covering my shoes and my jeans. Surely he was just out for a walk. I looked up one street and down another, pedaling faster and faster, straining my eyes through the grey haze of the morning, hoping to see his familiar shape up ahead. After passing vacant street after vacant street, the voice inside me grew louder and louder, ". . . you can't leave, you can't leave . . . you can't!"

There were no more minutes left to look. I hurried back to my brother's truck. John Charles and Jamie were waiting for me, but I poked my head in Phil's cabin one last time with a dashing hope. He was not there, and the chant began again in my mind. "Don't leave, don't leave, don't . . . !" The words were lost as I started to cry.

Dad was still on his tirade across the road, pacing around and yelling about not owning me anymore. "That's it! You're disowned. I mean it, you leave in that truck and I'm disownin' you. And that's that!" I could scarcely hear what he was saying anymore. I had stopped paying him any attention. I tossed my bike on the ground.

I threw my arms around Sara, and then Mom held us both very tight to herself. A salty sea of water rushed down my face soaking my scarred chin and my neck. John Charles joined in, hugging all three of us close to his chest with a mist in his eyes that looked as if it would quickly turn to rain. Jamie waited by the truck, kicking little rocks around on the ground with his shoes, pretending to look interested in something that was not there. Dad continued to drone in the background.

5

"Get in, Eartha. It's time to go," my brother gently said.

As we drove away, I waved to my mother and sister, watching their hands fly in the air. "Goodbye, Mom. Goodbye, Sara! I love you, Mom. I love you, Sara!" I yelled through the open window until they could no longer hear me. But I could not even whisper the words to Phil. He was gone.

When we neared Canada, I began to worry if we would have trouble at the border. Until then, I hadn't thought about the possibility of not being able to get into Canada without a parent or a legal guardian. At first sight, my learner's permit looked like a driver's license, but I didn't know if I could get by with passing for eighteen. I had only turned sixteen a few months ago. They could just tell us we had to go back. Sorry. Seventy-five miles for nothing . . . .

At the checkpoint, John Charles waited in the line of vehicles for our turn. When we got up to the officer, she asked to see his driver's license and the proof of registration and insurance for the truck. John Charles already had everything out for her to see. When it came to getting through the border, it was best to be prepared. "And I'll need identification for each of you." She looked over at me and Jamie. He fumbled through his wallet to find his license, and I quickly passed my learner's permit over to her. The officer matched the photograph on the card with my face and returned it to me with no further questions as she waited for Jamie. When he handed her his license, she studied it intently before giving it back to him with a bit of a frown. "And a record of the dog's vaccinations?" Once again, John Charles was ready with documents in hand, and after making sure they were up to date, she waved us through with a forward motion of her hand. "Go on. Have a safe trip."

The day was rainy and dreary. A flat tire, a stop at the Top of the World Highway, a few sandwiches later, and finally the outskirts of civilization began to spread out before us. We hit the pavement after six hours of gravel. Telephone poles marked the land along the road, and I watched their crosses fly by, playing with the ones way up ahead from time to time as they got closer.

John Charles wanted to make it to Whitehorse before we stopped to rest. By the time we got to Whitehorse, we were tired and hungry. It didn't take long before we started working on fast food time. He drove up to the side of a building where a sign was brightly lit up with descriptions of different foods and things to drink, pictures, and prices. A voice echoed through a speaker next to the sign. "Hello, welcome to McDonald's. Can I take your order?"

John Charles said, "Yeah, I'll take two cheeseburgers and a medium order of fries. What do you want, Eartha?"

"A grilled cheese sandwich."

"We don't have grilled cheese sandwiches." The voice didn't even sound disappointed.

What was I going to get? "What's on the cheeseburgers?" This was uncharted territory for me.

"Mustard and ketchup and pickles . . . but get something different if you want. They have chicken and fish sandwiches."

"I'll have a cheeseburger with a medium order of fries." It sounded all right to me.

"Anything else?" The voice echoed again.

Jamie said, "I'll get a Big Mac and a large Coke".

I started reading the list of beverages. So many choices, so little time, but I knew what I wanted right away. "I'd like a medium-sized vanilla milkshake, please." Now that sounded good.

John Charles agreed, "Make that two. I think that'll do it for us."

The voice said a quick thank you and then rattled off the total cost of our order. John Charles drove up to a window where we paid the voice—a young cashier in a neat uniform—for our orders. "Thank you. Please pull up to the next window." I looked inside where people were hurrying about everywhere making meals and fixing drinks. Our food was already being put in bags. Within a couple of minutes we were set to go, straws, napkins, and all. I was glad it didn't take as long as one of Mom's home cooked meals. We hadn't eaten much since we'd started out that morning, and we were all hungry.

Just outside of Whitehorse, we stopped at Wolf Creek Campground. John Charles set up a tent to share with Jamie, and Bogart moved to the front of the truck. I curled up in the back where he had been riding all day and soon fell asleep in a foreign country.

John Charles woke me up at about seven the next morning. I stretched my legs out, curled back up into a fetal position for a few minutes, stretched again, and crawled out of the back of the truck, rubbing motes out of the corners of my eyes. "Are we leaving now?"

"Yeah, Jamie wants to get on to Edmonton. If I get tired of driving, he can take over for awhile." Even though I had a learner's permit, John Charles wasn't going to let me drive. Mom didn't think it would be safe considering that my only practice had been on the gravel roads around Eagle.

In the evening, a rain began that grew harder and harder. John Charles continued forward for hours—long into the night—and the downpour had not relented. We had long stopped looking for a place to rest for the night. Motels were not a part of the travel budget for any of us, and the only way to stay dry was to keep driving or try to sleep in the truck. After another weary hour, John Charles finally said, "I need to pull over at the next stop and see if I can get a nap. Bogart can come up to the front, and I'm going to crawl in the back to stretch out. Hopefully, the two of you can get some rest as well. This rain is unbelievable." He opened the door and quickly ran around to climb in the back of the truck while Jamie pulled Bogart through the interior window to sit up front.

Jamie nodded off as he leaned his head against the passenger door. Bogart curled up between us. John Charles roused me awhile later, ready to get behind the wheel again. Bogart stayed with us while Jamie took a turn lying down in the back trying to rest. "Did you get to sleep?" I asked John Charles.

"Yeah, I got a couple of hours. It wasn't too bad back there."

Jamie poked his head through the interior window. "Not too bad? It's pretty rough every time you hit a bump in the road. I'm ready to switch with Bogart. Do you want me to drive for awhile?"

"If you feel up to it, go ahead. Even if the weather does clear up, we might as well keep going now that it's almost morning."

After a few hours, John Charles began driving again. By mid-day, we had reached the outskirts of Edmonton, and a billboard from up above screamed "Home of the World's Largest Pink Plastic Bunny Ahead!" Before long, we were at the bus station in the middle of the city. John Charles and I shared a fond farewell with Jamie. He had been a great traveling companion, but I was glad to see him go. The extra room in the truck was definitely a plus, but most of all, I was ready to have my brother and Bogart all to myself.

We spent the night in a campground near Red Deer. The sky remained cloudy, but at least the rain had stopped for awhile. John Charles set up his tent, and I slept in the back of the truck. In the morning, we woke up well-rested and eager to get to Georgia.

I was not allowed to drive—not even on the dreadfully straight roads of Kansas. My job was to keep John Charles from getting sleepy and to make sandwiches on the dashboard when we got hungry. He wanted updates about everything that was happening in Eagle. I had plenty of stories to share with him to keep him awake long into the nights.

I was looking forward to one of Grandma's southern dinners. Our main staples—other than fast food—were Raisin Bran, milk, peanut butter and jelly sandwiches, Top Ramen, instant mashed potatoes, and canned vegetables.

By the time we got to Blairsville, I had been so excited to see Grandma and Grandpa that I didn't know how homesick I was yet. Soon I was crying every day. I missed Phil and wanted to see him again, to have him hold me one more time, to have him say with his blue eyes how much he loved me. But the blue eyes were gone. I had left them behind.

CHAPTER THREE

"Done with the South"

DADDY WAS DONE with the South. He'd spent his time fighting the law and losing the whole way. There's a vague picture painted in my mind of people wrestling with concepts of justice in a generic clothing store. Daddy is there, before I am born, before I am conceived. Impressive stocky policemen move through the racks of clothing. Daddy has been called paranoid before. Schizophrenic. But in this work of art, Daddy is just scared. Damned scared. The salesperson waits. The officers wear guns. You can't see what's in Daddy's pocket. Daddy's told the story so many times before. So I know what's there. It feels as if I always have. Paraphernalia—that big long word that spells trouble.

And I wasn't at the Bible Study where Mama met Daddy. She had been raised strict Southern Baptist and hadn't recovered yet. Who knows why Daddy was there, but for some reason, he looked at her later that night and said, "I've been prayin' for a wife."

When Mama went to apply for the marriage license, they turned her away the first time. "I'm sorry, ma'am, but you need to know more about this man before you can marry him."

She knew his name was Al and that he'd been praying for a wife. So she figured out his birthday, his whole name, and went back to fill out the paperwork. Three months later, they were married. Daddy was living in a chicken house, a high school

10

dropout on his way up the ladder from mental institutions and jails. Mama was a quarter away from finishing her Master's in Education, a single mother of a four-year-old son, newly moved into a roomy house built by the hands of her own father. She sat among her high quality antique furnishings, in the house of her dreams, lonely as an orphan.

"I ain't livin' in that mansion a' yours." My not-quite-yet father stated emphatically to my not-quite-yet mother.

She put him in his place. "Well, I'm not moving into an old chicken house."

Daddy—always one to have a knack for deals—had invested in a faded turquoise 1957 one-ton Chevrolet van for $330. In decades past, it had served as a school bus for the black kids in North Carolina when segregation was still enforced by law.

For now, the van—a monster panel truck—was Daddy and Mama's transportation around town, but Daddy planned on driving it to Alaska. He wanted to take his new wife there in the spring.

At first, they camped deep in the mountains on the banks of Hatchet Creek, a place tucked away where few ventured to visit. When the chill of the new winter finally drove them to look for a home, they found a trailer for rent a few miles out of Blairsville off of Gum Log Road. Soon they were expecting a baby, and the not-so-carefully planned trip to Alaska was put on hold for awhile.

I was born several months later on a warm summer night in June. Mama and Daddy had friends over for dinner, and John Charles was with his dad. Mama started feeling as if she were going into labor, but she waited until they left so they wouldn't haul her off to the hospital. She'd taken that route with John Charles, but she wasn't in for the experience a second time around. This time, she had studied from a book, "How to Give Birth in a Bomb Shelter."

When Mama started seriously making noise, Daddy began yelling. "What's wrong? You sound like a dyin' calf! We gotta get you to the hospital right now! We gotta get you in the van! Get in the van, let's go!" But Mama was doing it at home this time—without any epidurals, doctors, or meds—and Daddy was along for the ride unless he wanted to put up a fight with a stubborn woman on the threshold of childbirth.

Daddy hadn't read any in Mama's book, but he knew about sanitation in medical situations. He put a pot of water on the stove, and when it started to boil, he took a Case XX knife out of his pocket and tossed it into the rising steam.

Mama said birth was the hardest physical work a woman could do—something that Daddy would never understand. Still he was there at exactly the right time to catch me, softly cradling my head before laying me down on Mama's belly. Soon afterwards, he cut the cord with his ever so clean knife, and the rest of the night passed with just the three of us at home, me all brand-new with Mama and Daddy.

The next morning, Grandma and Grandpa came to visit us for the first time. I was resting in a cantaloupe crate. Grandma threw a fit. "Ain't no grandchil' a' mine gonna be sleepin' in an old cantaloupe crate! Charles, let's go shoppin' for a decent crib right now!" She demanded and wailed at the same time.

Soon after I was born, we moved out of the trailer on Gum Log Road. Mama and Daddy had been offered a job managing Nottley River Campground several miles south of Blairsville— right off of Highway 129. They were long-time friends with the owners, Jim Bob and Annie.

Even though the park was near the highway, it was hidden behind a little forest of trees. Down where the campsites were lined along the river, it was easy to forget about the pavement and rush of traffic from up above. Daddy didn't have to pay rent for the cabin, and he had the keys to the public showers at the campground.

The job had a lot of benefits while it lasted, but when Jim Bob and Annie decided to move back into their cabin, Daddy needed to find another place for us to live. At first we stayed in a tent in one of the campsites, but Daddy soon learned that his friend Hubert had a trailer we could stay in for awhile.

Hubert told him, "You just stay there as long as you need to. There ain't nobody wantin' to move in this ol' thing any-time soon." Still Daddy and Mama hurried to get ready for their trip to Alaska. Mama was pregnant again, and the baby was due in mid-August. They had decided if they wanted to see

Alaska anytime soon, it'd be best to get there with enough time to settle in before the baby was out and about.

By the end of May, we were on the road. Everything we needed for the trip was packed into the 1957 Chevy: five stoves, cases of home-canned food, boxes of assorted traps, an eclectic assortment of odds and ends that Daddy and Mama thought would be necessary or useful to survive in the Last Frontier. Three spare tires rode on top of the van underneath a boat, which was covered by a canoe. Everything was securely fastened to the body of the vehicle with rope, wire, and bungee cords.

Daddy drove as many miles a day as he could, but he always stopped somewhere to camp in the evening. The front seat of the van worked great as a bed for John Charles. Mama and Daddy spent their nights in between covers spread out on the ground. I slept right beside them in a metal washtub that helped keep me warm and protect me from the wind. For fourteen days, we slept together that way—without rain.

I was just about to turn three. We were entering another country—far from the tall pine trees of Georgia and the sweet summer blackberries that dotted the hillsides. Here construction teams worked around the clock repairing the highway—the Alcan—through Canada and on into Alaska, using huge machines that hundreds of hands had helped make. As we drove through their worksites, my mind grew dizzy with the madness and determination of it all.

Daddy wearied as he wrestled the '57 Chevy through the worst of the detours. He grumbled, "If I'd realized the road was gonna be this bad, I'd never left Georgia." Once we hit the Alcan, he threatened to turn around a few times, but there was no way he was going back. Not now. He was headed for the city of Eagle—on the banks of the Yukon River—at the end of the Taylor Highway.

We spent our first night in Alaska on top of Polly Summit. The van's brakes weren't working right, and Daddy didn't want to test their last limits on the worst cliffs of the Taylor. The next morning, he fixed them enough that he thought they would get us on into Eagle. They continued to give him trouble the rest of the way, but luckily the road was dry. By evening, we were finally in Eagle.

For the first several days, we stayed at the public campground above the grassy airstrip, but there was a fourteen day limit. We would soon have to move somewhere else. Daddy and Mama started to get to know people as soon as they drove into town, and right after Guy Selman met them, he decided to take us on as one of his projects. He told Daddy about a place near his house where we could stay for the rest of the summer without having to pay rent.

You couldn't really call it a cabin. Guy said it had once been a mule barn. Even for mules, the place would have been a tight fit. The floor was partially covered with a few boards, with the rest good solid ground. A few crude pieces of furniture had been built into the corners and a couple of roughly constructed beds. There were places for windows and doors—but no windows or doors—and air shifted through the single room, along with mosquitoes, dust, and sunlight.

In exchange for labor and part of the produce, Daddy earned fifty dollars tilling up a garden in Guy's backyard. Mama planted seeds for green peas, beets, turnips, radishes, mustard greens, and spinach. She had grown up in a world where picking food that grew from a family garden came as naturally as filling up a cart at a grocery store.

Bartering worked for many things, but it would take money to buy some of the supplies we would need for the winter. When the Bureau of Land Management offered paid training for people in the community who wanted to learn how to fight wildfires, Daddy signed up for the classes. After several days of earning money, he was legal to work as a basic firefighter.

We were the *cheechakos*—the newcomers of Eagle—and most people didn't know how long we would withstand the trials of the harsh life in the Bush. The long days of light were now seven minutes shorter with each passing day. People hurried to get ready for winter, becoming squirrel-like as they worked and gathered. Daddy planned to stay awhile—a long while—and so he struggled to up the pace. We had journeyed to a precipice of the world, and Mama and Daddy were willing to look down at what was below. They had come too far to miss the view.

When I found out Guy's daughter, Martita, had the same birthday as mine, I stopped being quite as shy around her. Even though she was five years older than me, suddenly we had so much more in common. The two of us were going to celebrate together!

"What's that?" I asked her when I was at their house a few days before the party. Martita's mama, Martha, was dampening strips of newspaper in a paste and sticking them all over a box.

Martita explained, "She always makes a piñata for birthdays. That's how they do it in Mexico. How old are you going to be?"

"Two. I gonna be three."

Children of all ages showed up at the party. They took turns trying to break the piñata by swinging a stick at it, but as they were blinded by a kerchief covering their eyes, they spent more time beating the air. Finally one of the older kids gave it one last whack, and the contents quickly fell to the ground. Kids scrambled everywhere, fighting and shoving to pick up candy and peanuts as fast as they could. I was scared that I would get trampled if I tried to get anything for myself. Guy joined the kicking crowd and confiscated a few pieces just for me.

Daddy helped Guy set a net in the river in exchange for part of the salmon. Day after day, Mama preserved fish in quart jars using her giant pressure cooker. She cut large fillets into inch-sized cubes, packing them tightly into scalding clean jars. After adding a dash of salt or soy sauce for flavor, she covered the jars with brand new lids and rings that were boiling in a nearby pan of water. As she worked, she held onto the jars with a thick clean cloth so her hands wouldn't get burned.

After the jars were in the pressure cooker, they had to be steadily heated at a high temperature for an hour and half before they would be ready to take off the flame of the little Coleman camp stove Mama used for canning. When the time was up, Mama gently took them out, making sure that she didn't touch the top of the lids. She lined them up in neat rows, and as the jars cooled, the lids went "pop", "pop", "pop"— sealed to last for years.

Mama spent her days gardening, preserving fish and meat for the winter, and taking care of me. I had long since mastered walking. Running was my new thing. I trotted along ahead of Mama, daring her to catch up with me. At eight plus months pregnant, her chances were becoming slimmer by the day.

John Charles was the regular water hauler. The well-house— a tall building with peeling white paint and an old windmill on top—was not too far away. It had been built in the early 1900's and was still used as a major water supply for the town and the village. Mama often sent John Charles out with two empty five-gallon jugs loaded up in our little red wagon.

Daddy handed an envelope to Mama one afternoon after he had checked the mail at the post office. "We got a letter from Delbert and Nancy." They were old friends back South that had a little boy about my age.

Mama read it aloud. "It sounds like they might come up here this fall, doesn't it?" She half-asked herself. "It sure would be nice to have some Georgia folk around."

About a week before the baby was due, Daddy was called out to work on his first wildfire. He needed to get whatever work he could, and the BLM told him that if she went into labor, they would helicopter him back to Eagle. Mama was nervous, but the baby waited until Daddy made it safely home.

The nearest hospital was hundreds of miles away, but at least we were in a barn-cabin instead of a bomb shelter. Mama was so quiet during the birth that John Charles and I slept through it, but the baby woke us up right after she was born with her first wails of life. We all walked to the general store together the next morning, and Mama set her up on the produce scale to be officially weighed. "Eight and a half pounds," the storekeeper said.

Soon after Sara was born, Daddy and Mama started looking for somewhere to live over the winter. Daddy asked around town and found out about a place twelve miles out the Taylor where we could live. A shelter cabin had been built for workers and travelers to use on the Eagle-Valdez Trail back in the early 1900's. In years past, other families had dared to make it their home, but now it was empty and free for taking.

The cabin was buried in a valley amidst a wilderness of trees with piles of rock tailings from old mining days, along with a few abandoned doghouses, a dilapidated mule barn, two storage sheds, a cache, and an outhouse. Though people sometimes called the valley Gravel Gulch, that was definitively the name of the cabin. As much as Mama's name was Linda.

The cabin was sixteen feet by sixteen feet with no loft, but it had a complete wood floor, a window on each of the two side walls, and a sturdy bear-proof front door. The logs of the walls were tightly chinked with moss, and six inches of dirt sat on the roof for insulation.

A steep trail carved by feet from long ago started at the top of the road and led down to a creek in front of the cabin. Both sides were carpeted with blueberry bushes, pale yellow flowers of cinquefoil, and velvet green leaves of Labrador tea. Tall spruce and lanky white birch sprung up in the midst of the grey-green caribou lichen and soft spongy mosses.

A silence was impossible then—when we first visited—with the constant swarm of mosquitoes and the roar of rushing water, our voices rising and falling with the stream of sound.

CHAPTER FOUR

"Gravel Gulch"

WE MOVED INTO Gravel Gulch in the fall. The cabin was down in the valley, and everything had to be carried down the long trail, over the precarious foot log to get across the creek, and then up another little hill. I was still too small to help, and Mama was healing from having Sara, but Daddy and John Charles made trip after trip, and we began to settle in for the year.

The road would be completely covered with ice and snow in a month or two. Daddy started a tradition of taking us in on Fridays to get the mail, socialize, and prowl the dump for hidden riches. I loved looking for buried treasure in the trash, but John Charles hated it. Sara rode along on Mama's hip.

On one of the last Friday trips into Eagle for the year, dusk was beginning to fall. It was time to head back to Gravel Gulch, but the van's headlights had stopped working. One of Daddy's friends lent him a Coleman lantern to hang over a solid metal eagle that Daddy had mounted on the hood of the van a long time ago. We made it home just fine. But it didn't feel like we would make it home just fine when we were going around all those curves with just mountains on one side and cliff on the other. No guardrails.

I wasn't old enough to start school yet, but John Charles was about to begin the third grade. In rural Alaska, children must be taught at home if access to a public school isn't possible. The

Taylor Highway was officially closed due to extreme snow, ice, and windblown drifts for seven months of the winter. The only way for Daddy to get into Eagle was walk the twelve miles in while the rest of us stayed at home with Mama. He didn't have a snowmachine or a dog team, but he could always count on a ride back from someone who did, if not the same day, then the next.

Alaska Gateway Correspondence School—a free home school program—provided rural students with textbooks, supplies, lesson plans, along with a teacher's edition of each textbook. Michael Buck, the advisory teacher, had an office in Tok. He graded sample lessons and exams that we were to send in once a month. Every couple of months he would do a home visit out if he could get out to Gravel Gulch. Michael Buck also had to make sure that Mama knew how to correctly administer the Iowa Tests of Basic Skills. It had to be submitted every spring—a standardized test that showed where a student stood in comparison to others in the same grade across the nation.

John Charles was responsible for doing his lessons every day from Monday to Friday, but he could usually decide when he wanted to work on his studies. He often used the few hours of daylight for exploring outdoors, setting snares for rabbits, and joining Daddy on gold hunting endeavors. Mama always let John Charles have the weekends free to do chores and hobbies, but one day he forgot it was Saturday until he had already finished one of his lessons.

John Charles didn't just sit around waiting for things to happen. He worked for awhile building a sled for himself out of old lumber that he had found lying around the yard earlier in the year. Then he started figuring out how to go about designing and making a set of snowshoes to help him get through the woods when he was checking his rabbit snares. John Charles went out almost every day for long periods of time, hoping to bring home a rabbit or two for the evening meal.

He worked hard to catch rabbits in the woods on his trails. I knew from his stories that rabbits weren't quiet all the time like they seemed. If a rabbit got caught around its leg and wasn't dead when he found it, the screams would echo through the woods worse than a kid getting a good whipping, a sound that John Charles hated to hear. But when he brought home rabbit for dinner, we didn't have to eat fish. Jars and jars of fish grew quite monotonous as the days passed.

Time became ever elusive, vague and deceptive. Weeks passed where we went without a battery for our clock. The dark of night whittled away at the light of day faster with every passing week. But Mama had a wind-up timer from her summer days of canning that could be set for up to an hour at a time that she now used for baking, cooking, school lessons, and timeouts.

Aside from his studies and ventures into the nearby wilderness, John Charles spent much of his time hauling water and cutting wood for the winter. A 55-gallon galvanized barrel sat upright by the table in the cabin, which Daddy and John Charles struggled to keep full from the creek. Mama always worked to keep hot pots of water on the barrel stove and on the kitchen stove whenever she was using it.

We always needed more water. Just doing laundry was a never-ending chore. Sara was in cloth diapers, and I still had to wear them at night. Mama boiled the diapers in a big pot on the stove before washing and rinsing them clean. It was tedious, time consuming, and exhausting.

Mama proclaimed winter's arrival the first week in October, when snow finally fell to stay until April. Soon thereafter the road would close, so John Charles and Daddy spent several days going over the mountain past Gravel Gulch to get "burn-dry". The severely weathered wood—dry and damaged against the rising green—was excellent for firewood, easy to split and perfect for burning. They'd return at the end of the day covered from head to toe with little splinters of wood, dead tired, and hungry.

Mama always had supper ready, and we all sat down around one side of the round table in the middle of the room and ate three times a day—breakfast, lunch, and supper—without fail. The table was built around a stout post that helped support the roof so that the great log beams did not have to bear so much weight.

The dishwashing area was on the opposite side of the table from where we had our meals. Two industrial size metal salad bowls served as excellent washing and rinsing pans, with a dish drainer right beside the rinse pan. Besides for the table, the furniture also included an aging cabinet that reached to the roof with doors that actually opened and closed. A little pantry of sorts.

Mama spent a lot of time thinking about our food supply to make sure we would have enough to last us till spring. Regardless of how desperate our situation seemed, Daddy was stubborn, refusing to accept food stamps or public assistance from the government. If people in town volunteered to give us food from their garden or a hunting trip, Daddy almost always accepted the gift, but if he thought they were pitying him, he wasn't interested in whatever they had to offer.

Early in the winter, we got a load of carrots from the Kozariks, a family we had made friends with over the summer. The carrots were frozen with dirt around them, but after a good scrub they were ready to eat; rich and sweet and still filled with juice from the days of summer. We had them as snacks and as part of our meals over the next few days, and Mama canned 26 pints to save for darker times ahead.

Other people in town gave us moose parts that they didn't really care to preserve or eat. For hours—while she processed meat, fish, and vegetables—I diligently sat at the table cutting scrap papers into tiny pieces making imaginary green beans with a little pair of plastic scissors that belonged to John Charles. It took me a long time to get a pint jar full. Mama was glad not be bothered by a three-year old under foot. I wanted to stay busy and be good.

Sometimes more than anything, I longed to have schoolbooks and do lessons of my own to send in to Michael Buck, but I wasn't old enough yet to have a kit. I pored over my brother's books, looking at all the pictures. I was most fond of his health book—the "liver and brain" book.

We knew we might get to see Michael Buck if a plane buzzed the house real low, and a treat fell down from the sky tied to a flag. John Charles and I ran barreling down the mountainside digging in the snow where we would eventually find peanuts or candy. If Michael Buck was able to visit us, a few hours later we would hear a snowmobile, and he would be there all red-cheeked and smiling with some way to get me to talk to him. I loved sitting on his lap way more than any old Santa Claus. If I asked Michael Buck to send me a new box of crayons, some construction paper, paint, clay, or pencils, he always came through—except for coloring books. Those I had to make myself.

After the road officially closed, we hoped we would have enough wood to make it through our first winter in the cabin. A couple of weeks afterwards, Jerry Nelson—the last person to try to drive out—ending up getting his pickup stuck on American Summit, a few miles past Gravel Gulch. He had a snowmobile on the back of his truck that he was able to unload and drive back to Eagle so he wasn't stranded, but he had to leave his truck to be buried by snowdrifts until spring. Over the winter, we wouldn't have very many visitors at all – only one or two a month—usually a trapper or Michael Buck or John Borg. On one great day, Mr. Borg brought us fresh onions. We hadn't had anything fresh for several weeks, and Mama made us all onion sandwiches with her homemade bread and a dash of salt. We were constantly starved for fresh food of any kind during the darkest of those months when we were so isolated.

That year, when Mr. Borg didn't bring the mail out to us, we could count on Frank and Mary Lynn Robbins to drop it by when they made it into town. They lived 13 miles farther out the Taylor Highway than we did, but they had a snowmobile, so they could sometimes drive into Eagle even if the road conditions were bad. Mail day was a sight to see at Gravel Gulch. Everyone scrambled in crazy glee to claim what was rightfully theirs. John Charles was always eager to get schoolwork back and see his grades. I just screamed for anything to open. Mama perused letters from home, that southern place so far away, while Daddy skimmed the North Georgia News. Most holidays—Thanksgiving Day, Christmas, Valentine's Day, Easter—gave my grandparents a reason to ship a package or two of treats. We wouldn't always get them in time for the right holiday, but eventually the boxes would arrive, including case after case of disposable diapers—giving Mama a little break from the exhausting chore of boiling and scrubbing cloth diapers.

The process of doing laundry became more problematic as the weather got colder. At first, when the creek was running, there was plenty of water to wash diapers and clothes, and they would actually dry when hung out in the sun. As the winter progressed, John Charles would have to chop a hole in the ice with a hatchet to get down to where the water was trickling along. He then used a cooking pot that sat beside the hole to dip a five-gallon bucketful before lugging it up the hill to the cabin.

As the weather grew colder, this method became ever more challenging for John Charles. The water flowing underneath the ice was elusive and constantly moving. He could often hear water clearly running in a specific spot, but after digging down to its original source, the little spring could have fooled him, now echoing just a few feet away.

When the temperature was extremely low, Mama washed only what she absolutely needed. If there wasn't room in the house for the clothes to dry, she would hang the rest on the clothesline. After a few minutes, everything would be completely frozen. Later, she would go out to the clothesline, returning with slabs of ice-coated clothes as needed to thaw out and dry by the heater.

Although it could be difficult to get water in its liquid form, there was certainly an ample supply of it frozen. John Charles and Daddy kept trails shoveled to the outhouse, the creek, and the road, but if they walked anywhere else they would sink several feet right away unless they had on snowshoes. I weighed so little that I could walk right on the crust of the snow. Mama didn't venture far from the house, assigning John Charles the task of shoveling the snow away from the windows so we could enjoy what light was left during the days that kept shrinking away.

While the soft flame of the kerosene lamp still burned in the evening, after my sister had been put to sleep in her crib, I would claim my chosen corner of the house where a short sturdy shelf had been built by some past resident. Since we had moved into Gravel Gulch, the shelf had become mine, as a bedroom in a large house with multiple rooms becomes a child's room. Even though it did not belong to me forever, I owned it for a time simply because it was my space in the cramped cabin.

Mama had determined that it was strong enough for me to use as a bed, and I was absolutely thrilled with it. I kept my clothes and my few toys and books in cardboard boxes in the space underneath it, creating my own world in just a few square feet. Before the lamp was blown out for the night, I held up my hands and created shadows. My favorite of all was "the bunny ears". As my forefinger and middle finger hopped along back and forth, alive against the cabin wall and the ceiling, I knew I was not alone.

CHAPTER FIVE

"No More Cheechako"

I WOKE UP one dark morning and asked Mama, "When's it gonna be daylight all day again?"

"Not for a long time, Eartha."

I wanted it to sunshine so I could play outside, but I found plenty of indoor things to do that passed the time. I begged Mama into letting me rinse the dishes. I loved feeling like I was grown-up. I did chores to help out. I watched Mama and Daddy at everything, wanting to learn how to do things just like they did. When John Charles was working on his snowshoes, I decided to go about making a pair as well. I practiced sewing clothes the way Mama did to make them fit. I took care of my doll, Sara Elizabeth, just like Mama took care of her Sara, pretending to nurse her and change her diaper and bathe her.

We hadn't had visitors in about a month when Oscar and Dena Ingles, John Borg, and a few other locals came out on snowmobiles and brought our mail. There weren't any children with them except for Oscar and Dena's son, Eric, who was around the same age as John Charles. They were big boys doing their own thing. I was too eager for my mail to notice much of what was happening with anybody else. Plus Mr. Borg brought real apples, fresh ones, a whole sack of them, just for us. "Mama, will you start it for me? Please? Please?" I wanted to eat one right away. My teeth were too small to get a first bite, but after she got it going, I devoured it, as if I hadn't had fresh fruit in months, because I hadn't.

"Can I go spend the weekend with Eric?" John Charles wasn't ready for the visit to end.

"If you can get permission, I'll bring you back at the beginning of next week," offered Mr. Borg.

Mama wrote every spare moment she had over the weekend trying to get as many letters ready as possible for Mr. Borg to take into town when he brought John Charles back from Eagle. For more than a month, our only expenses had been a couple of dollars worth of postage. We had plenty of food and wood. When we could still make it into town, Mama and Daddy had bought the other major necessities that we needed for the winter: kerosene, batteries, wheat berries, dried pinto beans, whole-grain rice, oatmeal, sugar, salt, powdered milk, and canned evaporated milk, and of course, coffee and tobacco for Daddy. Daddy bragged from time to time about how he only spent $114 dollars to keep us alive that winter—with Mama as a witness.

Some people declare the cost of living in Alaska is expensive. But without water bills, electric bills, phone bills, life insurance, health insurance, car insurance, car payments, house payments or rent, bills from doctors and dentists, loan payments, or credit card payments we managed to live pretty cheap.

And then, what does distraction cost for the average middle-class American? For us, that year, the radio provided us with limited free entertainment. Without the fancy built-in booster, it would have likely not worked at all. After Daddy wired it up to an antenna and a few of Mama's pots and pans, the reception astonished us, especially when the weather was clear and cold. After listening to the news on a station out of Glennallen, we would pay close attention to the "Caribou Clatter" where people would send out personal messages to others who were hard to reach. The power source for the radio was the battery for the van, so we had to ration the radio in order for the charge to last. It was a special treat to be able to enjoy a few minutes of music along with "Caribou Clatter".

On rare occasions, when the reception was good, Michael Buck would let us know by radio when he would be coming to visit. The radio magically brought the world of Alaska into the cabin. One evening the governor told a story about someone in the Lower 48 who once said that Alaska was the last place on earth he'd ever want to live. The governor quickly retorted, "It's the last place left on earth I'd want to live either, and with any luck at all, it will be."

Our status of *cheechako*—that dreadful word—was diminishing as we continued to survive, albeit with the help of others. Although we had few visitors, almost anyone who stopped by brought some gift, and while Daddy never allowed us to accept assistance from the government, he did relax his definition of charity as people began to claim us as friends and not just outcasts who had drifted in from the Lower 48. On their way into town on Christmas Eve, Frank and Mary Lynn stopped by and gave us two moose roasts, candy, peanuts, popcorn, raisins, dried bananas, and hot chocolate mix, little bits of paradise that made the holiday warm and cozy, even though the temperature was –24° Fahrenheit. Slana Waller, one of the teenagers in town, was my bubble gum fairy. Someone donated a can of helicopter fuel to burn in the kerosene lamps as we were getting low. Mexican coffee came in the mail from Guy Selman, ginseng from Delbert and Nancy Greear in Georgia, and a Kodak camera from Grandma and Grandpa—sparks from afar that lit our dim world.

On our first Christmas in Alaska, I wanted to go to the bank back in Blairsville to see Santa. I had never seen him anywhere else. I told Mama, "Go to the bank, see Santa Claus, get apples, oranges, candy. Not Fairbank. That other bank."

Mama never told me much about Santa Claus. She did tell me that I might get some toys for Christmas. I said, "I already got some toys. I don't need anymore." My baby doll, Sara Elizabeth was enough. I loved her the best of anything.

Opening a package from Grandma and Grandpa took some patience, and I was usually not one for wasting any time when it came to opening any package at all (unless it was just another one of those cases of disposable diapers). Sometimes, it was agony to get down to the bottom. First Mama had to read the letter aloud to us so we would know what was happening down South. Under the letter, there was usually a layer of some dried food: stringy dried green beans called leather britches, wrinkly apple slices for pies, or fragrant sassafras bark for tea. This time, in the Christmas package from Grandma and Grandpa, there was a toy dish set just for me. I could use it to make whatever I wanted in the invisible world of imagination. I made tea for Mama as soon as I opened them and then started on coffee for Daddy.

Eventually, we got low on kerosene and salt. Daddy planned to walk into town to get them, but the weather kept getting worse the longer he waited. It was dangerous outside on foot. Richard Kozarik ended up bringing both items out on one of his round trips from Eagle to Gravel Gulch by snowmobile after receiving word that we were in a bad way. It's hard to function without light.

Whenever extra meat was given to us beyond what we could eat at the time, Mama would can it in the pressure cooker in quart or pint jars, whichever were empty at the time. I went from canning paper to canning snow, a much more efficient material to process in the midst of winter, where paper was valuable and snow was free. Mama never canned rabbits; they were a favorite fresh supper meal. Daddy had read somewhere that people couldn't live on just rabbit if they were to get stranded in the winter without supplies. After a delicious rabbit dinner one evening, Daddy said, "You might starve to death on rabbits, but you sure wouldn't die hungry."

That winter, we ate 64 of them in all.

Rabbit definitely beat fish. We weren't even halfway through the 98 quarts of salmon we ate over the winter when Daddy made a rule that we couldn't heat it up because the smell of cooking it was worse than just eating it cold. Then we stopped having hot fish and made fish sandwiches or just ate it plain scooped out of the jar onto our plates.

For some reason my baby teeth were terribly eroded, and Mama thought the fish bones would help me. She told everyone else to give me the bones from their serving of fish, especially the little round ones that made up the vertebrae. They were soft and easy to chew as a result of having been canned under pressure for an hour and a half. I ate them voraciously, calling them "favorite bones" for years after my baby teeth fell out to be replaced by my much stronger adult teeth. When we went back to Georgia for the winter when I was five, a dentist looked in my mouth.

He started counting cavities. Twenty-six of them in all.

"You gotta stop giving this kid candy. No gum either," he instructed Mama. I was furious. For a dentist, he sure was an idiot. I hardly ever got candy, only on special occasions. And Slana Waller only gave me bubble gum a few times a year. Or once in a while Grandma and Grandpa sent it in a package. Mama wouldn't even make a dessert with more than a cup of sugar in it, no matter what the recipe said. And Sara and John Charles had good teeth. They ate at least as much sugar as I did.

"That's more cavities than she's got teeth," he continued to drone.

Mama invented some horrible meat concoctions that I could barely get down. Thankfully, we had bread with almost every meal. Biscuits or slices off a loaf of bread made anything disgusting a little more bearable. I didn't like moose, but when she made moose patties and buns out of yeast dough, it was fun to eat. She called them mooseburgers.

We grew sprouts from seeds—alfalfa and mung bean—for something fresh, a rarity at Gravel Gulch during the winter. Even though our diet was bland and tiresome at times, Mama would always strive to make our food wholesome and substantial, even when she made desserts.

Mama was learning how to cook all sorts of food with limited supplies. She made everything from scratch. Sometimes her first attempts weren't always what she had originally intended, but we ate it anyway. I liked what she baked the best: whole-wheat yeast bread, sweet rolls, cookies, and whatever else she invented that had sugar and flour in it. Piecrusts gave her the most trouble until she learned a secret. Bear lard. It makes one of the flakiest crusts in the world.

Daddy ended up walking to town before the worst of the winter was over. We were going to need new lamp globes and soap soon, both of which we could have lived without for awhile, but, like all of us, Daddy was going stir crazy with cabin fever. He took advantage of the weather during a relatively mild spell and hiked the twelve miles mostly to get away from Gravel Gulch for a couple of days.

Just when we thought we were done with the worst of winter, February came around and smacked us in the face with day after day of subzero weather. Oftentimes we didn't know exactly how cold it was because our thermometer only read down to –40° F. The mercury would just hit rock bottom and sit there unmoving. The radio would broadcast the temperature in Eagle, –50° F, –55° F, –65° F, not counting the wind chill factor. For the first two weeks of the month, the thermometer was practically worthless; all we knew was that the temperature didn't rise above –20° F. Mama wondered, "Will the wood last till the cold's gone? Will the glacier bury the house? Will the baby crawl across the floor and get in the dirty diapers? Will the coffee last till the sugar runs out? Will the mail ever come?"

In the midst of it all, I was learning about a wider bigger world, all the way from dead presidents to the meaning of the universe. "Mama, what is God's name?" I couldn't figure it out by myself. What was Grandma's name? What was Mama's name? What was Daddy's name? I knew Daddy was really Al because Mama called him that all the time. So did John Charles. And Sara couldn't talk yet.

When I found out that George Washington's birthday was coming up, I was all excited. "Mama, can we make a cake and party for him? Please?"

"We'll just celebrate it by washing dirty clothes," she replied.

The next time John Borg brought the mail, Daddy received a refund check for $83 from the IRS from last year's income tax. Daddy had filed for unemployment earlier but hadn't earned enough money during his base period to be able to collect any of it. At least now we had some money. The weather had warmed up a bit, so Daddy decided to walk into town again and get some groceries, maybe even something fresh if the store had anything in stock! Richard Kozarik brought him back the next day on his snowmobile with a head of lettuce, apples and oranges, coffee, and a hundred pounds of flour.

Finally, a glimpse of spring appeared over the horizon of winter. On warmer days, water began trickling on the surface of the creek ice. Throughout the winter, the drama of the creek had replaced any desire for a television set. We closely observed how it changed from one week to the next. During the extreme cold, it turned into a miniature high-speed glacier, which grew upwards by the foot burying anything in its path. Two sleds, an ax, a cooking pot, a shovel, and other miscellaneous stuff completely disappeared. Mama gathered that it got around a half a foot taller everyday for awhile, eventually burying one of John Charles' sleds about six feet under the ice. John Charles rode his old hand-me-down bike on the flat sheet of ice, not even caring that he had trouble stopping because the brakes didn't work too well on the ice.

Then the frost on the windows started melting for good. A layer of frost had formed a good inch thick over the plastic. During the days in the deep of winter, some of it would melt when the fires were stoked in the barrel stove and wood cookstove, but at nighttime, it would just freeze again. And now Mama didn't have to chip the ice up off the floor to get out the door. In the winter, even when the fires were going, it was so cold by the door that ice and frost built up and never melted. With the warm outside air, Mama could wash clothes and hang them outside where they would actually dry instead of immediately freezing solid.

Every day became longer and longer. We started obsessing about being able to go into town soon. Almost six months had passed since Mama, Sara, and I had been outside of the little valley. My sense of distance was all askew. I believed that when the road opened we could just drive to town and see Grandma Beaver, who only lived five thousand miles away in Georgia.

I said to Mama, "We always go to Grandma Beaver's when the road opens, you just go right on past Andrew's house." Andrew was Richard and Terry Kozarik's oldest boy about my age.

Sara had no idea that any other world even existed. She had spent most all of her months in the log cabin, getting pushed in

31

her baby swing that hung between my bed and hers, nursing and eating carrots, growing teeth, learning how to sit up and crawl, and dirtying diapers.

Come the end of winter, Mama and Daddy were beginning to realize how rock bottom we were. Grandma and Grandpa had already been saviors in the diaper situation; the van held 432 dirty disposable diapers to haul to the dump on the first trip to town. Mama ended up asking Grandma and Grandpa for a short loan until Daddy could work a good forest fire. The van needed new tags, and Mama and Daddy hadn't gotten their Alaska driver's licenses yet. The nearest Department of Motor Vehicles was in Tok—173 miles away. The '57 Chevy guzzled gasoline – eight miles to the gallon. It hurt Mama's spirit to have to ask for their help, but she wanted us to have the van in legal driving shape. Month after month, she had stayed at Gravel Gulch, being a mother and a wife, and she was eager to see town again as soon as the road opened.

Oh, and it was exhilarating to see the road crew at work! I got caught up in the drama, exclaiming, "I sure am really glad to see that big yellow tractor!" On Richard Kozarik's last trip back to Eagle from Gravel Gulch, Daddy had given him the battery for the van to take into town and get charged. We were all ready to get the heck out of dodge.

First we stopped at the Kozariks, who lived in a sturdy plywood house right as you come into town. Daddy and Mama got along good with Richard and Terry. Daddy liked to work with Richard on projects around their house, and Mama had been pregnant the summer before at the same time as Terry. Andrew was slowly becoming my friend even though I was so shy it was hard for me to speak and play.

After visiting with the Kozariks, we went on into town to hit the grocery store, the garbage dump, and the Green Shop. Everything was secondhand and cost a quarter. A good T-shirt, a pair of trousers, a pretty dress.

At the end of the day, my mind was stretched out like a rubber band that's been holding too many things together for too long. Back at Gravel Gulch later that night, I could hardly sleep at all. I was anxious and tired. Thoughts raced around in my head like a hamster running around on its exercise wheel.

I'd finally get to sleep, but the same restless feeling would end up visiting me over and over again as I grew older.

After the road opened, we began to go to Eagle on Fridays. The snow was disappearing day by day, creating grand puddles of mud. John Charles was too busy to play most days because he had to finish his schoolwork and help Mama cut up a front quarter of a moose that was given to us on our first trip into town. It had been frozen all winter and had to be canned soon to keep it from spoiling. So I had to play by myself most days. I wanted Sara to hurry up and get bigger. She was growing everyday, but I certainly couldn't tell it then. I asked Mama, "Where will the baby go when Sara gets big?"

Easter came and went without much of a celebration, unless eating rabbit for dinner counted. Mama fried three of them. After supper, we ate jellybeans for dessert that Grandma and Grandpa had sent along with the money for our trip into Tok. More relevant than a holiday, there was plenty of reason to enjoy life. June twenty-first, here we come!

Mama started growing plants inside, cabbage, squash, peppers, and tomatoes. Daddy dug the snow out around one of the windows to add a small greenhouse onto the cabin. He built fires on top of the dirt in places where it was still frozen to help speed up the process, shaking his head and saying, "Thawing dirt to grow a garden, reckon I've done about everything now."

I made my own kitchen outside where I cooked cakes and pies out of mud and snow and washed dishes. Snow and dirt together at the same time baffled me. I loved it. I could put the two together and create dough with tiny specks that could be imagined into flour, spices, and brown sugar—whatever I needed.

The next time we went to town, the Yukon River had broken up. Mama kind of wished she had brought the camera, but, as she later said, "It wouldn't have captured the dizzy feeling you get standing there watching huge chunks of ice and snow and boulders push and crush and grind and whiz on by. It's impossible to capture the bigness of it all in a little bitty picture."

The glacier at Gravel Gulch was deteriorating, and water was running everywhere. Scents were coming back; the air had been almost completely odorless when everything was frozen because nothing could decay. We could see green grass beginning to poke through the patches of dirt, and flies and gnats and mosquitoes began to emerge. They had survived the winter as well.

That spring, two families that we knew from Georgia moved up to Eagle. We were still alive so they figured they could stand a good chance as well. They were ultimately lured by the familiar phrase that would tease so many others as well. The "Last Frontier" was, and still is, a tantalizing adventure for those not willing to become a part of the "rat race" of a more modern civilization.

In the middle of May, Chuck and Peggy Patrick arrived with their three boys, Jason, Abraham, and Solomon. Chuck griped to Mama about the Alcan Highway first thing. "Linda, when you wrote that the Alcan was rough, you should have underlined rough."

Delbert and Nancy Greear showed up a few days later with their boys, Ben and Jake. They had tried to make it to Eagle the fall before, but they got stuck in a blizzard in Wyoming and ended up having to spend the winter there.

With the arrival of the new Georgians, rumors began to fly. A few of the residents of Eagle began to think we were overtaking them. One day, the storekeeper asked Daddy, "How many more of you are coming up here anyway?"

"About 483," my dad joked, while maintaining a serious face. She stood shocked for a moment, but Daddy's inevitable grin soon gave him away. In any case, the town had gained fourteen Georgians in just a matter of one year.

Not too long after the road had opened Daddy was offered $100 to drive into Anchorage to pick up restaurant equipment for Frank and Mary Lynn Robbins. They were sick and tired of being out in the Bush. They had other plans now—the woods were for the birds. They wanted to start a business in Eagle.

Daddy drove Frank's army surplus rig, an old green truck as ugly as a pile of aluminum cans that have waited around a recycling yard a little too long. Somebody might poke fun now to hear that everybody around called the thing "Grumble Guts", but back then, there wasn't much laughter going on. It was cranky with some kind of truck disease that went all the way down to its truck intestines. On the way, Grumble Guts broke down with one ailment after another. Somehow Daddy kept getting it started, fooling around under the hood, Southern-cussing the whole time. Cotton-pickin' this. Cotton'-pickin' that. Dern it all. Dad-gum piece a' shit.

Along the way, my sister and I caught some kind of weird "Grumble Guts" sickness. We never got sick from riding in the '57 Chevy, no matter how many curves there were. But Sara threw up on my head and on my jellybean pants. And then I threw up on her head. We were *not* having fun.

We stayed with Jerry and Linda Nelson, a couple from Eagle who were living in Anchorage at the time. Their oldest girl, Katrina, was supposed to be watching me one afternoon while my mother was nursing Sara. We were smack-dab in the middle of civilization, and I decided to go exploring.

I wandered away from their apartment, and the next thing I knew I couldn't find anyone or anything that seemed familiar. I began panicking. I was lost. I began yelling over and over, "Mama! Mama! Mama!", but no one came. I cried as hard as my eyes would cry, until I began wailing, my three-year-old screams hurting my ears. The sun was out, and many grown-ups were playing a game in the grass up the hill from where I was screaming. I thought they could hear me—I was making plenty of noise—but they just kept on running around hitting a ball with a bat.

"Are you okay?" I looked up to see a pretty woman with short hair standing beside a car.

It took me a few moments to gather myself after all that crying and screaming. "I want my Mama." I still sobbed.

She let me get in her car, and I felt a little better, until she said, "We'll try to find your mama, and if we don't, I'll take you to the police station, and they'll help us."

Now I was really scared. Daddy had told a lot of stories about how he got in trouble with the police. They always showed up when you were naughty or bad. I didn't quite understand how it was they could help me. Suddenly, I felt that *she* might not help me at all.

"Where do you live?" she asked me.

"In a little log cabin between two mountains." Gravel Gulch seemed very far away, but I didn't know what else to say.

The woman drove along very slowly, stopping as she went to ask nearby people if anyone was missing a child of my description. She did her investigational work well and had soon found someone who was out looking for me. I wasn't going to have to go to the police after all! When they took me back to Mama, I felt like the sun had just fallen down from the sky to land right in my heart!

When we finally got back to Eagle after that harrowing trip, Daddy was called to work on a wildfire assignment. The rest of us were by ourselves at Gravel Gulch for the first extended period of time since we had moved there. Other than that, Mama had only had us kids for a night or two by herself when Daddy had walked into town during the winter for things that we needed.

Jean Boone, who used to live at Gravel Gulch with her husband Jack Boone and their children, drove out to get Daddy. He had to be taken to the airport in Eagle to fly out with the rest of the crew to fight fire wherever he was needed. Mama didn't like to drive the Chevy at all, but she wanted us to have the van at Gravel Gulch while Daddy was gone just in case we needed to go into town. Anything could happen out there in the woods: fractured bones, a bear attack, a bloody gash, fever that wouldn't break. We all felt safer knowing that the van was parked on the roadside above the cabin.

Earlier in the spring, Daddy had taken the plastic off of the window facing west to make an entryway for a greenhouse for us to use over the summer. The areas that he had patiently thawed into mud were now dry, and the dirt was ready for planting. Mama and Peggy Patrick planted summer squash, butternut squash, radishes, mustard greens, onions, and lettuce in the greenhouse. Daddy started a few trays of marijuana plants for himself.

Chuck Patrick dug up a bunch of ground about halfway between Gravel Gulch and where they had set up their camp. All of us kids would meet there with our mamas almost every day after dinner. Mama and Peggy planted beets, turnips, rutabagas, cabbages, green peas, bell peppers, beans, potatoes, and carrots. Jason, Solly, Abraham, Sara and I built giant cities in the loose piles of dirt around the garden, using rocks and sticks for buttresses.

Soon, we began to wage war with the mosquitoes, a battle from days of yore. Over the generations, primitive peoples have become what we call "civilized" in certain realms. Now you can buy all kinds of repellent for everything from mosquitoes to cockroaches at your local Wal-Mart. Or battery-powered rackets that zap the damned things to death. But up here, we weren't waiting for Wal-Mart to come to the neighborhood. We just wanted to get our hands on anything that worked better than "Cutter" or "Off". On days when the mosquitoes were thick clouds, they would run us out of the garden, even when we wore clothes that covered our arms and legs. We insanely waved our hands around, shaking our bodies constantly, hoping a few would get the point. But mosquito brains are very small, and don't forget the one-track mind.

The best weapon against the maddening crowd was the U.S. military insect repellent given to the firefighters working out in the wild. One can't be expected to live in the woods fighting mosquitoes with killer rackets as the trees blaze all around you. So when Daddy brought the little army green bottles home, we were ready to slather the stuff all over us. The bug dope was incredibly concentrated. We only needed to squirt a bit on the wrists and rub it on any of our skin that was going to be exposed to the air. You could taste the stuff in your mouth all day, no matter how careful you were not to get it on your hand. Even though it kept them from biting us incessantly, they still clung close nearby drowning our ears with their insupportable primitive whine for blood.

While we were waiting for the garden to grow, fresh edible plants from the wild were beginning to show everywhere. Mama taught me how to recognize the tiny red shoots of fireweed that popped up all over the hills. She showed me the tender new leaves of the dandelion plant and how to pluck them close to the ground. I scurried through the woods like a young squirrel in search of food picking wild salads for dinner. Later in the day, Mama liked to mix the wild greens with raisins and a little mayonnaise for dressing. Sure beat cold salmon from a jar.

We had been given a few chickens that ran around in the yard. They hobbled along on the gravel, clucking chicken songs all the way. I combed the yard every day for their eggs, hoping for at least one or two to give Mama for the next meal. "Mama, here's some flowers to send to Grandpa Beaver." I marched into the cabin with a handful of my favorites I had gathered on an egg hunting adventure. "And I found an egg for you!"

Mama told me about how much Grandpa would like all the flowers up in Alaska. Back in Georgia, he went on wildflower walks, studied them in books, memorized their shapes, took pictures of them, and perhaps dreamed about them at night when he was fast asleep. I thought he would like to see the dandelions. They grew up to two feet high here on tall, skinny stems that had been forced upward by the all-day daylight. Where he lived, the dandelions looked the same on top, but they huddled close to the ground with hardly any stem at all.

Sara couldn't make any sense about the seasons. In the winter, she had mostly slept when it was dark, but when the days began running into another with no darkness in between, her circadian rhythms got completely out of sync. She was often wide awake throughout the night. Mama tried her best to get Sara to sleep at nighttime, but Sara rebelled, and then napped much of the day away.

Sleep usually came easy to me then, even if the sun was still shining, after playing hard outside all day. Every day held another excitement, something new to build or create or explore. Often Daddy and Chuck were down at the creek below Gravel Gulch digging for gold. If Daddy was impatient, I couldn't go, but other times, he would take me along. Mama let me use one of her pie pans as a gold pan, and I would dig and play in the dirt, pretending that I would strike it rich.

I celebrated my fourth birthday, just days after the summer solstice. Mama made the best chocolate cake, from scratch of course. I got to invite the Patricks up from Star Gulch for a party.

Maybe Daddy and Chuck sat outside passing a joint back and forth or smoking tobacco. Maybe Mama and Peggy were in the background being philosophical together— wondering about all the what-could-have-beens and what-ares and what-will-bes. But inside the cabin, I was getting a grand sugar high with the two oldest Patrick boys, Jason and Abraham. We scraped the last bit of cake from the bottom of our bowls, knowing that we could have seconds! Sara and Solly crawled around together on the floor with frosting all over their faces.

Like last summer, Guy Selman wanted help with his fish net that he had set in the Yukon. Daddy was glad to work in exchange for salmon for us to eat and can for winter. We went to town almost every Friday to explore, visit, and work. While Daddy was on the river, the rest of us tromped around town. Mama learned where the top spots were to pick wild strawberries. The plants often dotted the ground in the grass around the airport and in overgrown lots. Soon after their white flowers bloomed, pea-size green berries would begin to form. As soon as they ripened, we were ready with our buckets. Even Daddy joined us when he could. We were starved for the berries we ate as we picked, hungry for desserts later, and eager for the jam Mama would make for the winter. Later, towards fall, raspberries, cranberries, rosehips, and blueberries would be ready to gather, but the wild strawberry, the one that opened the door to summer, ruled the wild.

Daddy was able to go out on two fires that lasted several days each. He also got paid to attend crew boss training, which meant that next season he could lead a crew of sixteen, with a higher rate of pay. With his summer earnings in his wallet, Daddy decided to ride into Fairbanks with the Greears to buy supplies for the winter. He came back with $700 worth of groceries, the basics to take us through the rest of 1979 and on into the winter of 1980.

For the time being, we had something fresh at almost every meal. Mama's garden had grown a field of treats full of vitamins, minerals, proteins and starch. For snacks, Mama would sometimes let me pick carrots or green peas that would never be for sale on some grocery shelf in Eagle. Mama studiously learned more about what could be eaten from the wild. Why waste something that's for free, right there, just because she didn't know?

She even mastered mushrooms. Puffballs and shaggy-manes were both edible and easy to recognize. You couldn't confuse a puffball with a poisonous one. Or a shaggy-mane. Puffballs were just cute little balls that were spongy when ready to eat. If you waited too long they were a blast to stomp on, sending clouds of green dust around your feet. The shaggy-manes created little mounds in the gravel alongside roads and other trails, silently announcing their arrival. When they first poked through they were said to be the best. Later they would turn an inky rotten black. Mama delighted in mushrooms. I thought they were the worst.

The sandhill cranes soon began flying in flocks overhead back South, forming their almost perfect vees against the flat sky, and a frost nipped the garden. Right away, we had a potato-digging party with the whole family acting as quality control. Make sure you don't miss a one, and look, here's another one!

Mama and I picked tomatoes, putting aside any that had the least bit of red on them. We wrapped them in newspaper and put them in a box under Mama and Daddy's bed so they could continue to ripen for a little while longer in the dark.

A lot of them were just green, so we ate fried green tomatoes every day for awhile. Mama made batches of green tomato pickles for the winter and one of the best pies ever. Slices of green tomatoes mixed with plenty of sugar and a few spices with a layer of crust on the top. A bit tart, but still sweet enough, and oh so fresh!

CHAPTER SIX

"Utopia"

MICHAEL BUCK CAME in from Tok with new school materials for John Charles—the fourth grade kit. John Charles was almost ten. I still wasn't old enough to do school. But Michael Buck always sent me most anything I wanted anyway. Except for coloring books. If I begged, he would sternly reply, "You can draw your own coloring books. And then, you can color them. Those are the best ones." He didn't believe in them. I sure did. I even found me one in the dump on a Friday when we were in town. A brand-new one, not even a mark in it. Sometimes you could really score at the dump. "One kid's trash is another kid's treasure."

Mama told John Charles that he didn't have to start his studies until the snow fell for good. He still had to carry wood and water though. He began to go out hunting almost every day, looking for squirrels to shoot for supper. When he brought any home, he would skin them and give them to Mama to cook. Mama fried them just like she fried rabbit, coating the legs and other parts with flour. John Charles started tanning their hides and saving the soft furs for Mama. Daddy liked to eat the brains. No one else dared.

John Charles sometimes killed wild spruce grouse for Mama to cook. When he caught one or two, we would eat them right away. On the fortunate day that he brought home several of them, Mama canned a few jars for us to enjoy over the

41

winter. So when Thanksgiving Day came around, we could have something other than moose. Something more traditional.

The spruce chickens were an easy target. They protected themselves by blending into nature and staying still. They could easily be seen on the sides of the road. The grouse would simply freeze against the gravel and dirt, a similar shade in color. No flight or fight here. Just freeze.

Mama would help me dissect the gizzards to explore what they had eaten right before they died. It was fascinating to explore what the grouse had eaten soon before it became our dinner. But the gizzards were no fun to eat. Just like moose gristle, chew and chew and chew. The best parts were the dark and white meat of the breast, the stringy muscles of the legs, and then finding the wishbone.

I discovered my brother's books pretty quick. As I had done the year before, I tried to make sense of them. One day, after picking mushrooms, I called Mama over to look at a picture of a mushroom in his science book. "Oh, that's an electric light bulb. But it does look like a mushroom, doesn't it?" She explained.

"It sure does look like one to me," I told her.

The Patricks, now the *cheechakos*, were stuck with having to find a place to winter. Luckily, Star Gulch was empty. Star Gulch was a cabin about a mile down the road from ours. The cabin, even smaller than Gravel Gulch, didn't seem to be owned by anyone in particular. If it had been, no one was writing up a lease or expecting payments for rent.

About a mile up the Taylor, a newcomer named Brad was quietly moving into an even smaller and more isolated cabin. It could not be viewed from the road. And cabin can mean a lot of different things. This place had no windows, a dirt floor, and you better not be tall if you want to practice good posture.

Nobody was standing around to collect rent. Brad, the only black person I'd seen in Eagle, had come in during the summer and wanted a place to stay. He wasn't leaving. He decided the place would do.

So we had neighbors on both sides of us. The population in the Bush was booming. A whopping eleven of us were soon to be snowed in until April—maybe March if we were lucky. Two families of five from Georgia, and one African-American from nobody knew where.

Grandma and Grandpa were so far away now. Since we had moved to Eagle, I hadn't been anywhere except for that dreadful trip to Anchorage. "Mama, I wish we lived close to Anchorage, so Grandma Beaver would be closer." She couldn't make me understand where all the packages came from: the cases of Pampers, the presents, the clothes and boots.

"Mama, what was it like in the old days when you were a little girl? Did your mama have a wood cookstove and a kerosene lamp and a scrub board?"

"Well, no. We had electric lights. And running water right in the house."

I couldn't picture a light in Gravel Gulch that you could just turn on with a switch. Sometimes when I played house, I imagined what a faucet was like. "I got one of those electricity water things, with cold, hot, and warm, you just turn the handle, and it goes on, off, on, off, on, off. See, Mama?"

I often sat and watched her while she sewed. This fall, she was making mittens for us. Mama spent hours drawing the patterns out until she got them just the way she wanted before she started sewing. I liked it when I had to hold my hand very still on sheets of paper for her to trace around it. The pencil always tickled a little as she drew, but I knew if I moved at all my mittens might not fit me right. I knew they would keep me cozy warm as she stuffed the linings with down feathers from birds. Just when I thought she was all done, she told me it would be just a little bit longer. She still had to trim the edges with soft fur.

I wasn't considered old enough to go out with Daddy on most of his outdoor adventures. And I was a girl. Daddy was in charge of the wood, the water, trapping and hunting, but John Charles sure did a lot to help out. John Charles kept shooting squirrel after squirrel and catching every rabbit he could snare so we would have more food to eat.

As for income tax purposes, Daddy was the head of the household. He was not to be reckoned with on home issues as well. When he got mad, you needed to be quiet. Sara got a little more leeway because she couldn't even talk yet, but I was supposed to know better by now. It was Mama's job to take care of me and my baby sister. And cook. And clean.

When Mama was kneading bread one day, I asked her, "Can I help?"

"Sure, you can knead part of the dough." She pulled a little piece off for me and showed me how to push my hands down real hard in the dough. "Do it like this so it will rise up nice in the pan. I reckon you'll turn into a real helper for me."

"I'll be a helper, but not for you—for Jason, I guess."

"Why Jason?" she asked.

"I'm gonna marry Jason." I was determined.

"Oh, yeah? Why?"

"Cause he does everything I say."

I always wanted to tag along with Daddy and Chuck to look for gold, but they didn't usually want little kids underfoot, whether or not they were girls. They were digging a hole down below Gravel Gulch trying to reach bedrock. The foundation of the bedrock would keep the heavy gold from falling any further. Because the ground was frozen solid with permafrost, they would build huge fires where they were digging to thaw out the dirt as they went. It was slow going. The last thing Daddy wanted to do in the middle of that whole operation was to have to babysit.

One afternoon, Mama decided to bundle me and Sara up to take us down to see how far they had gotten. When we got there, I looked at Daddy standing in the hole with a grin on his face and a sparkle in his eye. The hole was already over Daddy's head. He was sure to strike it rich any day. Just as soon as he got down to bedrock.

We hardly ever saw Brad. I called him Black Brad back then because everyone else did. He was darker than any of the Natives in Eagle Village. His hair was all wiry and never seemed to grow much. He kept to himself. Nobody ever brought out mail to him. He didn't even have an address in Eagle. He only went into town twice the whole winter for things he needed.

We only went up to see how he was doing once in a while because he seemed to like it by himself. We found him making a ring out of thin copper wire under the dim light of a lamp. He had a whole workshop set up in his cabin making his copper rings, twisting the shiny metal wire into all kinds of pretty shapes.

Brad was about as skinny as anyone I'd ever seen. The few times he did come down to Gravel Gulch to visit, he didn't talk much. He sure praised Mama's cooking though. He'd eat whatever she cooked up, except for bear. Then it didn't matter how hungry he looked. "I just cain't eat 'im," he would sadly say as if the bear was his only brother or something.

Brad used about one gallon of kerosene for his lamp to our fifteen—in a house that didn't even have windows. He must have spent an awful lot of time in the dark. And he didn't have to eat much food to stay alive. Daddy exaggerated, "I could carry on my back all he ate that winter."

If anybody asked Brad where he was from, he acted like it didn't matter. "The farther away from home you are the better. The only reason I quit going is I ran out of road." He called the place Utopia.

Chuck was around more than Peggy and the boys. Daddy and Chuck worked together mining the gold hole or trapping for furs in the woods. If they didn't get nuggets in the delirium of gold fever, they would at least get some money for marten furs. Marten furs sold for about forty dollars apiece. It always seemed more likely that Daddy would bring home another glossy brown marten than a sparkling gold nugget. He would have to skin the dead animal and tan the hide before it would be ready to sell. Not as exciting as holding a chunk of gold, but the soft furs put more food on the table for sure.

The year before, we hadn't had any neighbors at all. This year we had old friends from Georgia just a mile walk down the Taylor. The Patricks brought more than new life and energy to the woods. The world around us was less foreboding. If an accident happened or supplies dwindled, we wouldn't have to worry anywhere near as much.

On November 10, Daddy would be 38 years old. And company was coming! The whole Patrick family walked up to have supper and birthday cake. Mama made one of the meanest birthday cakes ever, and Jason and Abraham played with me all day. Sara and Solly practiced toddling. Solly loved to eat butter, and if we had any, Daddy would quickly demand that it be put it away before the Patricks got to Gravel Gulch. "Hide the butter, the Patricks are coming!" Out would come the margarine. If we had any.

John Charles was almost six years older than me and Jason, the oldest of the Patrick kids. As he did much of the time, he occupied himself on that invisible line between the two groups. Sometimes, when the adults were all laughing and telling stories, and us younger kids were playing, he faded into the background so much that you could hardly see him at all. Maybe he was thinking about Eric back in town.

Just two weeks later, we all went down to Star Gulch for Thanksgiving dinner. The days were short now, but that didn't keep us inside then. Sara rode on Daddy's shoulders and John Charles pulled me on a sled. Mama walked along, grateful to have her hands free of any children. When we left, it was just coming daylight, at about ten o'clock in the morning.

Star Gulch was about two-thirds the size of our cabin and even tinier with all ten of us in it. Dinner was delicious! We ate several fried squirrels, fried rabbit, mashed potatoes, buttered green peas, rye bread, sprout salad, gravy, pumpkin pie, and chocolate cake, and gave thanks to God for having food and family. Afterwards we visited for awhile longer, and then began trekking home at three o'clock in the afternoon. The dark had already set in until the next morning. The whole walk back to Gravel Gulch, I kept looking upward at the star-speckled black ceiling, wondering what God was doing up there.

Later that winter, I got to spend one of the few nights of my childhood away from my parents. Daddy had agreed that I could stay overnight at the Patricks.

"Peggy, when are we going to have to wash our hands?" I asked as we put our pajamas on before bedtime. Mama always made us wash up in a little white porcelain bowl and brush our teeth right after supper.

"I don't see any reason for y'all to wash your hands at night. Y'all 'ul just wake up with 'em dirty anyway," she rationalized. "You can wash 'em in the morning."

I slept with Jason, talking in whispers late into the night until we finally fell asleep. I awoke to the smell of pancakes, the semi-sweet mixture sizzling in circles on Peggy's griddle. Back at home, we almost always ate oatmeal or biscuits and gravy for breakfast.

That afternoon, after a good shift of play, their big dog Shoney pulled me back to my cabin on a sled with Chuck in the lead. I had talked Chuck out of an old manual Royal typewriter so I could learn to type. I clutched it carefully on my lap and Shoney plodded along. I wanted something more to do at Gravel Gulch than play with Sara or practice cutting with paper scissors. I had already mastered cutting paper dolls and clothes out of old catalogues. I was sick and tired of coloring by myself without any good coloring books. I knew typing would keep me good and busy.

As we covered the mile home, the dark was all around us, everywhere. My whole world was in front of me. I had a new tool to help fight the drear and gloom of the ever-pounding winter.

Unlike those trips we made to Eagle in the summer on Fridays—when I returned all anxious and lonely—visits to the Patricks gave me renewed energy. I had played with Jason and Abraham back in the North Georgia mountains a long time ago. I now knew that other people could just drive up the Taylor from Georgia and live right down below Gravel Gulch.

To this day, when I travel back to those moments to visit those times and places, I can still feel the bewildering sense of being intertwined with nature. Then I brushed so close to God—a Spirit that no religion can capture on paper. Surely, Alaska can be cold, irritable, and violently cruel. But when we returned home from Star Gulch on dark afternoons, she became a blanket for the soul—warm and cozy.

Nevertheless, the frightening moments of the dark and the isolation became almost unbearable. Usually the presence of Mama and Daddy reassured me that all would be okay, but there were times during the winter when I wanted to face the outdoors alone. "I'm practicing my bravery," I would tell my mother some evenings as I stood by the door. I would wait there, solid and staunch, until I gathered the nerve to face the fear head-on. Then I would run full force up the little trail to the outhouse. All the while, my heart pounded madly; my mind frozen with fear of the unknown. Then, after what seemed a very long time in the outhouse, the same mad dash back to the house. Once indoors, I would have such a sense of relief and wonder how I had possibly survived.

When I awakened during the long nights, I could never summon enough courage to make myself go outside. Instead, I would stumble to the children's "toilet"—a size number ten coffee can with a hole cut in the plastic lid so my bottom wouldn't get hurt. One day, when I was big enough I could use the five-gallon bucket that Mama and Daddy had on the other side of the room. But not yet.

John Charles was disgusted by the whole deal. "I never used it. Not once." He always chose to go the outhouse regardless of how cold it was or how bad the wind was blowing. John Charles could remember the "mansion" he used to live in before Mama met Daddy. He knew what it was like to have electricity and running water. And he wasn't four years old. He was ten. But I used the little coffee can, moving quietly in the dark through the nightly ritual. I didn't like the way the cold crept into my bones so viciously and quickly that it caused me to shiver for long minutes after returning to bed.

Mama and Daddy couldn't keep my fear at bay. I had something built in me, a silent voice that told me I needed to be careful with myself so that I didn't get hurt. But Sara, still just one year old, was bold and reckless, often falling from somewhere high, spilling hot water on her bare skin, or bumping into the stove. The nearest doctor was almost 400 miles away, in Fairbanks.

Sara loved to climb up onto the trunk that I used for a seat when I was playing or studying or working. Mama took her down again and again, but Sara just kept on climbing until the day she lost her balance and tumbled straight to the floor. Her mouth hit the sharp metal corner, and blood poured from her upper lip. One of her baby teeth had been fully knocked up into the tissue of her gum and was no longer visible. Mama stopped the bleeding as fast as she could and got enough butterfly closures out of the first-aid kit to bandage up the wound.

Sara's tooth grew back out but instead of being white it was the color of a grey winter sky.

If some accident were to happen that Mama or Daddy or time couldn't fix, there would be no doctor or nurse, no modern technology to reverse the damage done. Nature could be intensely awesome at times—inspiring a dread and ultimately demanding respect. Living at Gravel Gulch made us all see the value of fear in life, that sort of fear that one might have for God—a wonder or reverence, rather than terror. I learned intuitively to be cautious. I fiercely believed in God.

John Charles wasn't afraid to go out by himself for hours if it was only –20° F. He knew to dress warm: a snowsuit on top of blue jeans and long johns, a coat or two over that, two pair of socks in his boots with wool liners, a face mask, a hat, or two. Then he would be off to check his snares or hunt for food.

Mama didn't worry about him too much. He knew better than to go out at –45° F or –50° F. After a couple of weeks of –60° F, the temperature shot up to –30° F. John Charles decided to take advantage of the not-quite-so-dreadfully cold weather, so he packed up his usual lunch, a brown sugar and peanut butter sandwich, and headed out to see if he'd had any luck.

When he reached the spot where he liked to take a break and eat, he was overheated and sweaty because of hurrying. He got terribly cold and couldn't get a fire going for almost half an hour. His fingers were too numb to grasp a matchstick, but he was finally able to get it struck by using his teeth to hold it.

John Charles diligently focused on his schoolwork when the weather was at its worst. He wished to make the most of the warmer days, exploring the mountainsides, checking his snares, hopefully bringing a rabbit home, something for supper.

Just because he was able to structure his lessons around the temperature and the light during the middle of winter, didn't mean he could slack off. To complete a year of school, nine checkups of sample daily lessons and all tests had to be submitted to the office of Alaska Gateway Correspondence School. He had to get his checkups done by the end of May. Otherwise, he would be stuck with finishing them over the summer.

Michael Buck, the advisory teacher for the region where we lived, would grade and return them either through the mail or in person. He visited us every couple of months, keeping an eye on John Charles' progress and my potential as one of his future students.

During one of his visits, he brought picture cards for me to try to identify. He kept flipping the cards over as I gave my quick answers, showing me the word on the back.

"And this? What's this?" He kept prompting me as he turned the cards.

I knew the picture was a big animal. I guessed, "It's a moose!"

Michael Buck chuckled kind of like people who pretend to be Santa Claus. "No, Eartha. Good try, though." It was a rhinoceros. What was I to know about rhinos?

We almost always knew when to expect Michael Buck. We would either hear about it through the "Caribou Clatter" when we listened to the station or by the sound of a low plane circling over the cabin. When he flew into Eagle, he always had the pilot fly real close to the house so he could drop a surprise for us.

When we heard the familiar buzzing, John Charles and I would run outside without even thinking about putting on extra clothes, waving wildly in the air. We carefully kept our eyes on the path of the plane so we could know where to look for whatever fell from the plane. The last time Michael Buck had buzzed the cabin, he was on his way back to Tok from visiting Delbert and Nancy Greear to check on Ben's progress with school. They lived several miles down river and couldn't get into town easily.

Delbert and Nancy wanted to let us know that they were going to dogsled into Eagle in a couple of weeks and that they would come out and see us. They had given Michael Buck a note to drop down to us. It was in a plastic sandwich bag with a bright yellow streamer attached to it. John Charles and I scrambled madly to dig it out and bring it back to the cabin. Besides for the message, there were a bunch of peanuts in the bag for us to enjoy.

Mama said spring was the time of year between March and the beginning of mosquitoes. The Taylor Highway would officially be open on April 15, but as soon as the road crew plowed out as far as Gravel Gulch we could drive into Eagle. We were all ready to see town again, and Sara laughed and laughed as Daddy rocked her back and forth in her little push swing.

We were able to go into town the first week of April. The '57 Chevy was full to the brim with garbage from over the course of the winter. I was looking forward to playing with Andrew again, going to the library, and seeing what I could find in the dump.

Daddy was able to sell three of his marten hides for money to buy new groceries in Eagle, including some fresh fruit, apples, oranges. He always needed something from Jack Boone's hardware store. Boone had kerosene, wicks for lanterns, propane, chainsaw parts and chainsaws. And lamp globes. Daddy had a strict rule about lamp globes. If I broke one, I'd have to pay for it. There were times he'd pull that belt off incredibly fast, slap it together, and say bend over. He could be in an angry mood sometimes. And of course, I knew what came next, ". . . and they cost eight dollars, so whenever that grandma a' yours sends you some money, you gotta buy a new one."

Before we left to go back to Gravel Gulch, in that hour when the night can become a bit sad, we went to the Eagle Library, and I got to check out books to read when we got back home. I could read lots of words. Mama had read a chapter from the Bible every night before we went to sleep with me sitting right beside her for months on end. I would look at the words as she read, learning a few here and there. And Michael Buck had sent me a few storybooks to practice reading. I wanted to read all at once, everything, so I could see what was happening in books without just looking at the pictures.

By the time we went into Eagle in the spring, Sara was learning how to say new words. "Go." "Away." "Truck." "Gold." She copied Daddy, pretending a tube of Chap Stick was her bottle of gold, holding it up and turning it sideways, just like Daddy did when he wanted to see the flakes he had found magnified by the water in a one ounce bottle.

Daddy just knew that he could strike a vein of gold if he got lucky. Chuck and Peggy had moved closer to town for the summer to set up a camp, so Chuck didn't spend much time in the gold hole. Now that it was summer Brad was out and about, and like everyone else, he had to eat. So he worked with Daddy to hunt gold. They didn't ever find the nuggets Daddy dreamed about, but at least they didn't have to go buy dredges or helicopters or bulldozers. For Brad, gold simply meant food. He traded some of his for 75 pounds of beans. Brad was thinking about the basics of making it through next winter.

One year in Alaska had been plenty for the Greears and the Patricks. They planned to go back South as soon as the summer was over. Daddy got the idea in his head that he was going to take us to Georgia for a year so we could have a break from -60° weather in February. He was thinking ahead.

Daddy scrounged together as much money as he could for the trip. He sold his traps for $100 and the barrel stove for $75. He got another $75 for his twenty-two rifle, along with $200 for a boat he had got for a good bargain awhile back.

In August, we packed up most of what we owned in the '57 Chevy, leaving behind all the things we wouldn't use in Georgia. What we didn't take with us, we stored in the shed up near the outhouse at Gravel Gulch.

Since Gravel Gulch would be empty after we left, Brad decided to move into it while we were gone. Daddy was planning on us returning to Eagle the next summer. He couldn't just expect that Gravel Gulch would be empty then. But Brad said, "I'll take care of all yo' stuff. Don't you worry none about it. Ain't nobody gonna get in that shed and mess with yo' stuff. When y'all wanna live here again, I'll be goin' on back up the road."

CHAPTER SEVEN

"We'll Be Back"

MAMA AND DADDY didn't have to pack the van as tight as last time since Daddy had sold so many things in Eagle for gas money. They were able to leave enough headroom that we could crawl on top of everything when it was time to go to bed. Mama and Daddy slept longwise in the van with Sara in the middle. I had plenty of room to stretch out alongside the bottom of their feet. John Charles was still short enough to sleep in the front seat where we rode during the day.

Before we left, Mama had to figure out something to do for John Charles that would keep Daddy from throwing a big fit about public school. Daddy had a habit of ranting about the whole system of public education, throwing around the word "brainwashing" with about every other breath when he got on the topic. He wasn't into our pretty little dirty brains getting cleaned up without him being the one in charge of the brain bath. John Charles was about to start the fifth grade, and I needed to start kindergarten.

It was decided that John Charles would go to public school and that I would stay at home. School was optional for kindergarteners anyway. I had waited so long for a school kit, but if we could go to Georgia and see Grandma and Grandpa, I wouldn't be too disappointed.

I had long since graduated from cutting paper with my little kid pair of scissors that wouldn't even go through a piece of cloth. I had happily banged hours away on the Royal typewriter that Chuck had given me. I could almost count all the way to Mexico. I could read. I'd learn plenty enough on the way. It would be a grand field trip. I didn't need a school kit!

We didn't have to race to get back to Georgia like we did on our trip up North. The roads that led into the North Georgia Mountains were open all year round. And Mama wasn't pregnant. We were all excited about stopping at Liard River Hot Springs in British Colombia. Daddy had been talking about it even when we were back in Eagle.

I didn't know what I was going to use for a bathing suit. It was easy enough to find socks and shoes and regular clothes in the thrift store, but people didn't use bathing suits much in Eagle. But before we left town, Mama had managed to scrounge one up for me and Sara.

After a few days on the road, we reached Liard. As we pulled into the campground, Daddy said "That water's gonna feel derned good." He found a site he liked, a little farther away from the others, and we jumped out of the van, ready to head for the hot springs.

Mama put Sara's bathing suit on, and I wiggled into mine. Just a little ways from the van, we started walking down a boardwalk heading back in the woods. "Mama, how far is it?"

"About a quarter-mile, I think. It's not far."

We got there faster than I thought we would. I wasn't expecting that the water would stink like old eggs. Mama said it was naturally supposed to be that way because of sulfur.

The water was deep, and I didn't know anything about swimming. It's hard to learn how to swim when the water only gets up to about 35° F in the middle of summer. All I could do in American Creek was play games to see how long I could hold my feet in the water.

At first, I just sat in the water on the stairs leading into the giant bathtub. Then I got brave and walked down a few stairs. All at once, there was nothing under my legs but water. I panicked. I had to keep breathing. Then, I felt the ground with the bottom of my feet, but I was all the way underwater. I tried to keep breathing. All I could get in my lungs was water. I kicked and kicked and tried to scream. I just got more water in my mouth. Mama was there right away. "Be careful, Eartha. Sit up here where you won't fall." After that, I obeyed without fail, sitting on the lower stairs. I wasn't about to repeat that experience if I could help it.

On the road, we got to eat things that we usually didn't eat in the Bush. We still ate oatmeal for breakfast most of the time, but every once in awhile Daddy would buy cold cereal and a big gallon of milk. He liked Cheerios, Raisin Bran, and Corn Flakes. When we stopped for lunch, we usually ate sandwiches: fresh banana slices with mayonnaise, tomato slices with mayonnaise, or cheese sandwiches with mayonnaise, even canned pineapple slices with, of course, mayonnaise. When we stopped at night to camp, Mama always unpacked the Coleman stove and everything she needed to make us a hot supper before we went to bed.

The next big stop was Aladdin, Wyoming. Only fifteen people lived in Aladdin, and they were plenty proud of it. On their way up to Alaska, Delbert and Nancy had met a couple that lived there. Jim and Pearl were the main reason that Aladdin existed. They owned the general store right near the post office. They kept the whole town stocked with bologna and cheese, churning out slices with the biggest bologna-cheese cutting machine ever.

Instead of driving on to find a campground, we stayed in a nearby field. Jim told us we might run into a few wild Indians. "There isn't any reason to be afraid of them though." I wasn't scared of wild Indians for a minute, but then he added, "Just watch out for snakes." I didn't think wild Indians were out to kill little girls, but snakes were a different story. And just to prove Jim right, we saw a rattlesnake not far from where we had just set up camp.

For a change, we had bologna sandwiches with cheese and mayonnaise. Even though Sara and I weren't about to go out and play in the field after seeing that snake, at least we didn't have to listen to Daddy griping about where we were going to park for the night. Aladdin was a bit out of the way for the RV'ers.

It took us three weeks to hit the border leading into Georgia. Grandpa and Grandma were about to see two-year-old

Sara for the first time—the blue-eyed blonde of the family. Sara liked being with Grandma and Grandpa just fine if Mama was around, but if Mama and Daddy wanted to go somewhere without us kids for awhile, she would scream nonstop until Mama returned. Sara freaked out anytime Mama wasn't with her. And she wasn't about to fall for any trick when I tried to tell her that it was just Grandma.

We needed a place to stay right away. Daddy's first idea was to ask Hubert if we could stay in his trailer again. "What do you think about me renting that trailer of yours for the winter? It's just sittin' there empty."

"Ya'll just move right on in. I sure ain't usin' it for nothing." The trailer wasn't too far from Blairsville, but still off the beaten path. Most of all, it had enough room for us to live without being all cramped together. And it suited Daddy just fine. No electricity or running water except for a stream nearby.

Hubert lived in overalls and walked around barefoot everywhere he went. He was great fun. "Did you know I'm your Uncle Hubert?"

"Really? Nobody ever told me I had a Uncle Hubert before."

"Look at your toenails there. See how they grow under instead of out? You inherited those from me for sure." He showed me how to peel them off with my fingernails just like he did.

Even though Uncle Hubert's didn't have running water, the trailer did have a bathroom with a big tub in it with a drain that worked. Mama decided the best way to do laundry was to put a load of clothes in the tub and fill it up with water from the spring and add a little soap. Then she'd have me jump up and down on them for fifteen minutes, and they'd be ready for a rinse. After wringing them out, she'd fill up the tub with water again, and after fifteen more minutes of jumping up and down, they'd be ready to hang on the line.

Mama and Daddy often visited Jim Bob and Annie at Nottley River Park. Rachel had already been born before we moved to Alaska, and they had a new baby boy named Jesse. Sara toddled around with him, talking and using about every new word she learned.

I wanted to be friends with Rachel, but when she acted as if she knew everything, I didn't feel like I was having much fun. One day when we were working on playing together she said, "You know, I invented the kaleidoscope."

I peered into the deep ever-changing shapes of colors falling upon one another. "You did not." Who did she think she was? Einstein?

"Yes, I did." She argued. Maybe she had made a cheap one in some arts or crafts class. I sure hadn't ever made one, but I knew they'd been around long before Rachel was ever even born.

When we got back home, I started itching all over. "Mama, look. What are these?" I worried. I hadn't been running around in a patch of busy mosquitoes. Mosquitoes didn't even usually like to live in places that got as hot as Blairsville.

She looked at the spots I was scratching. If a bump had ever wanted me to scratch it, I started in on it right away. I didn't care if my nails made it bloody; it felt too good to have the itch and indulge in giving it due attention. I didn't even mind peeling off the scabs later if they bothered me. "Eartha, it looks like you caught chicken pox from Rachel or Jesse."

"What?"

"Chicken pox. It makes you get bumps, and if you are exposed to it, it's easy to catch."

"Why did you let me play with them?" She wasn't making any sense. She didn't even seem worried.

"Well, usually kids get it sometime in their life. Better now than later. Once you get it once, you won't ever get it again because you'll be immune to it." Mama was definitely the grownup here. "Don't scratch those bumps. If you do, you'll just get more. They'll heal up a lot faster, and you won't have anywhere near as many if you can be good and keep your hands away from them."

No matter how many mosquitoes bit me in Alaska, they never spread around if I scratched them to pieces. I got mad at Mama. "Why did you let me play with them?" And then she explained it to me again, but all I heard was ". . . it'll be over soon, just don't scratch them."

I couldn't stand the itchy bumps, but I didn't want millions of them all over my body. Sometimes, I found myself uncontrollably giving in to the urge. Then I would remember they spread all around if you did. So I would hold my hands really tight together and try not to think about them. And like Mama said, after a few days, they went away and never came back.

On Tuesdays, Daddy and Mama took us girls to Murphy, North Carolina to the flea market. John Charles never got to go on Tuesday because he was in school, but Daddy went every Saturday as well, so John Charles had his fun then. Murphy had a famous flea market and people came from all around looking for what they might like to barter or buy. Daddy was a flea market expert. If he came across fifty cases of plastic wrap for a good price, he'd buy them all and sell them individually at our stand with the price marked up for profit.

On busy days, the flea market was crowded with people. Like so many others, Mama and Daddy came for the excitement of finding a good deal. Daddy wasn't just there to find a deal though. He was there to make a sale. He kept busy looking at other tables and on tailgates for things that he thought he could buy and then sell at our table and earn a profit.

Old men boiled peanuts in big pots over stoves made out of fifty-gallon barrels. I liked to hang out around the stoves, looking at the bubbling juice, wanting to see if I'd be able to taste a few of them to make sure they were good enough to sell. Some of the men whittled away on pieces of wood, creating shapes like boats or tops that would spin really fast.

"Whatchya whittling?" I asked one of them while Daddy was talking to someone else nearby.

"Whittling? A girl yo' age know the word whittling? How's that for ya?"

He looked over at the man sitting beside him. "This girl here know about whittling."

"Any girl yo' size know about whittling oughta have a knife of 'er own." He handed over the one he had been using. I looked at it for what seemed a very long pause, at the light brown surface that had sporadic dashes of a darker brown running along its length. "Try it out." I picked up a scrap of wood lying on the ground and gave it a few strokes with the knife, shaving away curlicues, just like happened when you sharpened a pencil.

He looked up at Daddy and without skipping a beat said, "You care if she have that knife? She'll make fer a good whittler."

Daddy surprised me as much as the man did. "You sure you want to part with it?"

"She'd be a good whittler, and if she ain't got a knife of her own, this 'en here's just her size."

"Well, I reckon." He looked at me and said, "But what'd I tell you about using a knife?"

"Always cut away from yourself." I knew the answer as fast as he could pull his belt off when he got mad about something and wanted to let you know.

CHAPTER EIGHT

"The Summer That Never Was"

WE STARTED THE trip back to Eagle when spring was well on its way. This time, being on the road was exciting in even more ways. We knew that Jim and Pearl would be welcoming us in Wyoming with bologna and cheese. And only a few days after that, we could go to Liard River Hot Springs!—the best stop of the whole trip.

Every night we searched for a campground that met Daddy's expectations. Daddy hated "Kampgrounds of America"—a chain of campgrounds that catered to expensive RV's and upscale tourists. He didn't like to stay anywhere fancy, but KOA's were completely off the list.

At suppertime, we dragged out pots and pans, the Coleman stove, plates, silverware, cups, and food. And that was just to make dinner. Then we had to put everything back in place real tight like it was when it came out so we could sleep on top of it all like we had traveling down to Georgia the fall before. John Charles still spent the night in the front seat. Sara and I barely fit in the back with Mama and Daddy.

Daddy didn't like to get out of the van to go pee at night. He slept next to a hole in the side of one of the wooden panels of the van that had once been cut out for a stovepipe. He used it as a bathroom whenever he could. The further away we were from big rigs with fancy names like Discovery and Explorer and Wanderer, the happier he was. He wanted a little privacy, for God's sake.

60

That's why he liked to get to know people like Jim and Pearl. Besides for free bologna, they welcomed us into their home for supper, like we had lived next door for years. After living so long in Aladdin, with its frightening population of fifteen, I guess they had grown to know their own neighbors pretty good.

"Go ahead and camp over in that field you stayed in last fall," Jim offered. He didn't own it by any means, but he figured nobody would mess with us. "Just watch out for snakes. Don't let those girls wander off too far by themselves."

Daddy would have camped in a field any night over a campground. Especially one that came with a hot supper beforehand and no one coming around demanding to collect a few dollars for the spot. And he could pee any old way he wanted.

As the miles flew past at a speedy forty, forty-five miles an hour, the van kept trucking along. If Daddy drove much faster, we all started to wobble a little too much for comfort, and rattles came from places we didn't want to think about too hard. Not that the '57 Chevy didn't have an ailment or two now and then.

We were on the road, in the middle of a pouring rain, when suddenly the windshield wipers stopped working. Daddy immediately got off the road.

"Dad-gummit!" It was still early in the day. We weren't anywhere near an auto shop. Daddy's brain started working overtime. You could see crinkles all the way up his forehead.

"I need some string. John Charles, Linda, do you know where any string is?"

Of course, we had string with us. Just where it would be was another question. But that was the central focus of the moment. Sure enough, string was found. Daddy tied a fair length of it to the wiper on the driver's side, and then he told John Charles to hold it. John Charles always rode right behind Daddy in a little seat that was put there especially for him.

Then he instructed John Charles to pull on the string to make sure it was positioned right to move the windshield wiper a few strokes. It worked! We were back on the road in less than ten minutes.

A monotonous dialogue—if you could call it that—began between Daddy, the speaker, John Charles, the silent "puller", and the swish of the solitary windshield wiper.

"Pull!" Daddy said forcefully when he had to strain to see through the water running down the windshield.

John Charles pulled on the string.

"Pull!"

John Charles pulled.

Swish.

We rode otherwise in complete silence. Pull, swish, pull, swish, pull, swish. I counted numbers in my head. You couldn't even see what was outside from where I was sitting. No cows. No oil pumps. No trees. Just water running down.

When we finally reached the border between Canada and Alaska, Daddy had us all good and nervous. He had a stash of marijuana hidden in a closed interior vent overhead. We always dreaded crossing the border fearing that the officers would decide to search our vehicle. They had the right to do so with no apparent reason at all, but Daddy mustered his confidence and kept up with the conversation.

"Turn off your vehicle, please," the officer said briskly. We were all piled into the front of the van, except for John Charles who sat in his backseat.

"Well, I would, but I won't be able to start it without somebody givin' me a jump if I hafta turn it off right now. I'm havin' to run off the battery. The alternator's burned out." Getting a new alternator was one of the next things on Dad's to do list.

"Keep it on then." The officer went ahead through the formalities of asking all the basic questions over the sound of the engine. We passed inspection, and were allowed back into the Last Frontier.

If the officer had made us turn around, it would have probably taken us a good long while to get back across Canada. All four of the spare tires had already been used. As it was, we made it the rest of the way without another flat tire, and the '57 Chevy limped into Eagle near the end of June.

We set up a summer camp right off of the road that led into the village. John Borg owned the land and had given us permission to stay there until winter. Daddy and John Charles set up our big blue tent, a sturdy canvas structure that kept us from getting soaking wet when it rained. We all slept in it, us kids on army cots, and Mama and Daddy on their bigger bed that they made over a low bed frame covered with a piece of plywood. For the next two months, it rained almost every day. The tent stayed damp and cold from the drizzle that clung to the outside of the canvas.

Soon after we arrived in Eagle, Benny Juneby, a Native friend of ours stopped by our camp early one morning. He was so excited to see us that he woke us up. "I knew you would come back, Georgia, I knew you would come back!" We were no longer *cheechako*. Benny had given Daddy the nickname Georgia when we had lived in Eagle before, but he knew Daddy was done with Georgia now that we'd returned. The Last Frontier was home.

I hardly ever cared how muddy or wet I got, as long as I didn't have to be in the tent. John Charles and I spent almost every afternoon deep in the woods to the left of the camp. We measured, sawed, and hammered out forts that we thought were better than any old tent. We banged away the days and our frustrations, warming our chilled bodies with the arduous physical labor required to construct a private home for just the two of us. We could have easily been miles away from any adults of the world. Our diagrams and plans could not be rivaled. We were the architects of the neighborhood. I had complete conviction in our projects because John Charles was brilliant. I worked hard to be a good helper.

For a time, John Charles and I were in the right place at the right time to truly enjoy one another. He was free from school and hunting for the season, and I was big enough to be included in his outdoor world. We had no need to build castles in the air. Just a little fort of sorts where we could abandon our damp beds in the tent as much as possible during the day. The dream pushed us forward as we played and worked. John Charles and I measured wood, hammered nail after nail after nail, and proudly noted our progress every day. During those hours, a peace and strength ran through the forest like water over stones. And like those rocks deep in the wilderness, we were ever so slowly becoming new shapes.

I was also learning about the rewards of conviction across the road at Vacation Bible School in an old building that the owner allowed groups of missionary youth to use. They always came into Eagle during the middle of the summer to hold classes for local kids. A gold star just for memorizing a verse in the Bible that almost sounded like a tiny little song? And free cookies and Kool-Aid for good participation? It was like heaven.

I didn't always trust John Charles though. I thought he'd lost his mind one night when he kept poking me in the ribs over and over. "Eartha, wake up, wake up! Eartha, there's a bear right outside!"

"Shut up." I fell right back into sleep.

"No, really, there is."

"Shut up." I was still lost in sleep as I said the words.

The next morning, I realized that he had been dead serious. I was completely frustrated with myself for having missed the excitement. The bear had explored our camp, just feet from where we slept, and I hadn't even gotten a peek at it. Daddy had gone out after it and shot it once in the rump, but it still got away.

"Meat right on the doorstep, and we missed it," Mama said—as if we had a doorstep.

Mama's gathering instincts had kicked in full force once again. Berries were ripe, fish had recently started to run in the Yukon, and hunting season was open. There were berries to pick, jam to make, and fish and meat to can. She took advantage of every opportunity she could possibly manage.

Someone talked her into canning a caribou that they had killed "on the halves", which meant that they would get half of it back in sealed jars, preserved for the winter. We ended up with 30 quarts for ourselves, along with the ribs and bones, which Mama boiled to can in jars as broth to use in future meals.

Early that evening, when Mama had just finished making dinner, the fear—the terrible one that even Mama couldn't make go away—visited. Daddy and John Charles were gone at the time. Mama had just taken a huge pot of rich caribou broth off the campfire. I took a seat on a five-gallon bucket of water to eat my serving of fried potatoes, and Sara started looking for a place of her own.

Sara spied the pot nearby right away, and before anyone could say anything different, she sat down on it. Within a split-second, the lid slipped, and Sara had fallen rear end into the broth. All I could hear was her screaming, worse than any I'd ever heard before. I froze with fear. Then I saw Mama's eyes and knew I had to move. She couldn't work alone, and I was the only other one in the camp. "Open that bucket!"

With intuitive strength, I managed to pry the top off of the five-gallon container of clean cool water with a frantic hurry. Mama instantly dunked Sara's body down in it, once, then twice. Then she started stripping off all of Sara's clothes. I could see pieces of her skin on her shirt and pants. Mama yelled at me, "Get Loren and Carol! Run! Run! Fast!"

Loren and Carol lived in a house just across the street and up a few yards from where we were camped. I took the short-cut trail, running the maddening distance as my mind shrieked, "Fast, fast, faster, faster!" My little baby sister's skin. Those pieces.

"Come! Help! Sara's burned! Bad! Help! Come!" Carol and I raced back to the camp by the shortcut, while Loren sped in their pickup around to the front of our camp where vehicles could drive in and out. Loren drove us the three miles down to the clinic in Eagle Village. Sara screamed Mama's name the whole way, as if Mama wasn't holding her up in her hands, as if Mama wasn't there at all. She just kept screaming like that, over and over, "Mama! Mama! Mama!" I rode right beside them with the fear balled up inside my chest, a huge lump that wouldn't let me catch my breath right. When we got to the clinic, I stood by and watched her get treatment, wanting so badly for her to stop hurting.

The clinic was the only medical facility for both the village and the city. The community health aide worked hard not to panic. "What happened? Linda, we have to keep her still. Lay her down on her belly. Yes, right here." The room smelled like medicine.

First, the health aide ever so carefully removed any extra pieces of flesh that had been severely burned. After that, she put an ointment over all of the raw places and dressed Sara all over in brand-new white paper. As the nurse worked, I pointed to the red places where the skin used to be. "What's that?" I asked, full of curiosity. I was able to breathe better now that we were in the clinic.

The health aide replied, "That's her meat underneath where her skin was. But if we take good care of her, she'll grow new skin back over it. We just have to keep her really clean and take care of her until she gets better. She can't play around on the ground at all for awhile."

I babied her for weeks afterwards, loving her as strong as I loved my mother that awful day when I had gotten lost and found in Anchorage. Sara was more precious to me now than ever before. I would do anything I could for her, *absolutely anything*, to help her get better. Every morning, we took her to the clinic to get new ointments and fresh dressings. The clinic didn't have a doctor, but the people who worked there knew a lot about how to help people in crisis. I wanted to cry when I saw Sara's burns when she got her dressings changed, but the health aide kept telling me that Sara was healing without any problems and not to worry too much. Just to keep her clean. Make sure you keep her clean.

Sara couldn't wear clothes while she was healing, but she was proud of her paper skirts. They made her pretty and clean and white. She wasn't allowed to toddle around like she did before the burns because she had to stay clean so she wouldn't get an infection. So I pulled her around in our little red wagon, hour after hour, forgetting about forts in the woods that had to be built and Bible verses that should have been memorized. And as the weeks passed, she grew all new skin, and only the scars of that terrifying day remained on her backside.

Around the same time in another part of the town, the truest of horrors happened. This one was irreversible, a loss beyond compare. Children often got hurt in Eagle, especially ones who were accident-prone like my sister. But they weren't supposed to die. Even if they were really, really mean. But Jason Mittenium was hardly ever even mean. One day he suddenly disappeared. Soon afterwards, the word had spread. He had drowned in the Yukon, trying to swim to the other side. I heard that someone had dared him. He was only a few years older than me. Just a kid.

They dragged the river for days, hoping to discover his body. They weren't able to find any trace of it there, but if you go to the local library you will find tributes to Jason's honor. Or if you go to the Eagle Cemetery, you can find a tombstone bearing his name. Perhaps you would like to place a flower or two there for him. He can never have too many.

I had turned six earlier that summer. Even with the tragedies so close to home, I never questioned that God had given his only begotten Son so that I would not perish, but have everlasting life. All I had to do was believe in Jesus. With all my heart. No matter what happened. Or I might die forever.

The chance rainbows that arched over the camp, the calm voices of the Bible schoolteachers, and the quiet evenings when I fell into sleep alongside of my family reassured me that life was good. Even so, I knew to be extra-vigilant so terrible things wouldn't happen.

The "summer that never was" was almost over. Cody—the last goldminer of the season—was getting ready to head back to the Lower 48. He had toughed it out the whole way, but he had no plans to see what winter had to offer.

Cody had been camping out in a tree all summer out at American Creek Campground. When I first saw his setup, I asked him, "Why are you living in that tree?" I was puzzled. I had never seen a grownup staying in a fort built up in a tree.

"I need to get some good pictures of a bear that's been prowling around," he explained.

Cody was from Chicago. He had decided to come up to Eagle for the summer hoping to strike it rich.

Daddy had driven through Chicago when we were traveling across the Lower 48. I had all kinds of questions for Cody, wanting to know what it was like to live in a big city.

"Where'd you live in Chicago?" I asked him.

"In an apartment. On the fifty-first floor."

"What? No wonder you live in a tree!" Suddenly, Cody's camp made a lot more sense. How could he ever live right on the ground? The fifty-first floor?

I often tried to determine how high or wide distances were by "daddies". That was about six feet. But I couldn't use my daddy ruler to measure that high up—*that many daddies each standing on top of the other?* Even in the tree, Cody was already a daddy and a half up in the air.

CHAPTER NINE

"Michael, Row the Boat Ashore"

BRAD WAS STILL living in Gravel Gulch when we got back to Eagle, but Daddy had planned on us camping in town until fall. When we needed to move back into Gravel Gulch, Brad had already found another place to spend the winter. He wouldn't have to go back into that dreadful dark windowless structure up the Taylor. Harold Nevers, who had a mining claim three miles down the road, had given Brad permission to move into a cabin that was on the property. The cabin was just a few yards off the Taylor, with windows and a solid wood floor. Brad was our only neighbor now.

Michael Buck soon brought schoolbooks and materials for the year. Now that I was six, I would get a kit for the first grade. Even though I hadn't missed anything by not being in kindergarten given that there were so many things to do back in Georgia, I was in desperate need of expanding my activities in the narrow world of Gravel Gulch.

Michael Buck gave me a reading test, asking Mama, "Where'd this kid learn to read?"

"She just taught herself how." Mama replied, shrugging her shoulders.

He said that I could read well enough that I didn't need to do the first six months of Reading. I had started learning to read at four years old. I felt like I owned every word that I mastered, a dominion that opened up kingdoms far beyond the valley.

Even before I was officially enrolled in correspondence through the Alaska Gateway School District, I knew that words and numbers were like free tickets. Tickets to other places. At first, when Mama would slowly read the nighttime chapter out of the Bible, I would ask what little words were. Then I began to see every "is", the straight thing with a dot on top and the squiggly thing that looked like a squiggly snake.

After my own set of boxes came from the school district, almost all I wanted to do was schoolwork. I even begged Mama, "Can I take my math workbook to bed just to look at it a little more?" I had already fallen in love with reading words, but Math was a completely different story filled with numbers instead of letters. By the end of September, I had already finished half of my book that was supposed to last all year. Math was straightforward and logical to me, like Reading. I could easily get a grasp on using numbers or recognizing words.

I never wanted to do my Social Studies. What did Social Studies have to do with anything? I did like the pictures of Thailand and thought, "When I grow up, maybe I can move there." Mama said they never had any snow in Thailand, just a lot of water.

I had developed quite the Southern accent from my parents. My schoolbooks didn't seem to take into account the advantages of being able to drawl like a down-home Georgian. How could "dog" possibly rhyme with "log"? My spelling book insisted that it did.

"Mama, is it supposed to be 'dawg' and 'lawg' or 'dog' and 'log'?" I knew how to spell and read the words just fine, but pronunciation could be ridiculous. The whole idea of phonetics seemed like an unfair punishment.

Aside from school, I couldn't quite get the lesson of distance straight in my head. Our three trips across the United States—from Georgia to Alaska, Alaska to Georgia, and then back to Alaska—confused me even more. One night while we were eating dinner, a vehicle drove by up on the Taylor, tooting its horn as it passed. We looked out to see who it was, but it was driving too fast. John Charles said he thought it was a truck, but he didn't know whose. I said, "If it's blue with white, it might be Grandma."

John Charles said, "Oh, that's impossible. It's way too far away."

"We were down in Georgia, playing with Shannon, remember? How do you think *we* got here?" I flatly replied.

Sara was just over three now, figuring everything out. "It's gonna turn winter someday, and the snow will come up out of the ground." And when it first snowed, about a foot in all, she said, "I told you the snow would come up out of the ground."

The snow meant the end of woodcutting for Daddy and John Charles. They had been spending most days hauling wood for us to use over the winter or to sell in town for cash. Daddy cut all the wood down with a chainsaw, and helped John Charles drag the long heavy sticks of wood to the road and load it up in the van. Daddy cut good wood. He only sawed down dead trees that were already dry and would burn easily. Oftentimes, Daddy and John Charles would travel over an hour out the Taylor to Liberty Creek where they knew they could find dead trees left behind from an old forest fire.

George Beck would buy just about as many cords as they could cut because he was elderly and couldn't do the job himself. Mr. Beck scared Sara to death. He had a sense of humor that Sara hated. Every time we delivered wood to Mr. Beck, the old guy looked down at Sara and jokingly threatened, "I'll put you in a gunnysack and keep you for good." He really was only teasing, but Sara thought he was the meanest man in the whole world.

Daddy hadn't been able to go out on any wildfires over the summer, but he had sold enough wood so he could buy some groceries and kerosene for the winter. Our stash of food was slimmer than it had been the other winters we had stayed out at Gravel Gulch. And even though you couldn't see it, all three of us kids grew a smidgeon of a smidgeon taller every day. While it seemed ever so gradual, we needed more calories as the months passed.

Marten would sometimes roam throughout the woods and while their meat was seldom eaten and generally considered inedible, they were known for their long slender frames coated with strong soft fur. Marten furs were always in demand. Daddy planned on trapping the weasel-like creature over the winter and tanning their skins so he could trade their furs to the General Store in exchange for food or supplies in case we got too low. One fur—with its skin completely tanned and ready for market—could be worth up to forty dollars depending on its size and condition.

Road maintenance for the Taylor Highway was officially discontinued early in October. Some hunters and people going to the bar would pass by once in awhile, but the road was treacherous in many places, especially at the bridges where ice would quickly build up on the sides. We heard a rumor that Cody had gotten stuck going over American Summit on his way out and that it took him six hours to get out. He had slid off the road after getting distracted by a bear chasing a caribou.

In November, Daddy tackled one last trip into Eagle. The road had been officially closed for over two weeks, but he thought the '57 Chevy would be able to make one last trip into Eagle before spring. We made it into town just fine, hitting all of our favorite spots, the P.O., the grocery store, the thrift store, the dump, and the Kozariks.

On our way back to Gravel Gulch, we got stuck on "Brad's Hill". The hill was a treacherous climb right up the Taylor from the mine cabin where Brad lived. Back then, Brad was always known as Black Brad. But Brad's Hill didn't have anything to do with skin color. We just said it belonged to Brad.

The van ended up spending the winter in the ditch covered with snow. Before we left it behind, Mama told me, "Eartha, you can take something from mail. Pick what you want." We would have to walk over two miles to get back to Gravel Gulch.

"Can I carry the package from Michael Buck?" Mama looked at my skinny six-year-old frame. Her eyes shifted to the box. "I can do it, please, Mama, please?" I begged. I knew that he had sent us something unusual. I could tell by lifting the box. Even though it was bulky, it wasn't all that heavy. It couldn't be books. And it was addressed to all of us, not just John Charles. There had to be something in it for me. I wanted to solve the mystery. I didn't care about anything else in the van at the moment.

"Why don't you look for something else? That'll be hard to carry all the way home." Mama didn't know how bad I wanted it.

"I'll carry it the whole way. I promise. I can do it just fine."

Mama was a good teacher about promises. She didn't take them lightly. If you made a promise to Mama, she knew you were serious. But she meant business about them. Promises weren't made to be broken. They were made to be kept.

"You'll keep your promise?" She asked.

"Yes, I promise." I knew I could do it. I was strong enough.

As we walked along the Taylor, I stumbled in the snow, shifting the package to maintain my balance. One foot in front of the other. I had made a promise to Mama that had to be kept, but that wasn't what mattered. I wanted to know what was in that box.

When we got home, I opened it right away and found several markers of different colors and circles of paper that were as thin as tracing paper. Michael Buck included a letter explaining that we could draw pictures on the papers, and when we sent them back to him, he could have them turned into plates. Michael Buck truly had special powers.

Mama said there was enough paper for us kids to make two plates each. I drew one of a house with a yard in front and a road going by and another of a cup covered with elaborate designs. John Charles carefully wrote out his name using his best cursive inside a perfect circle that he had made by drawing around a mixing bowl. Sara quickly scribbled two works of art. Mama spent hours carefully lettering a plate with a little sentence that meant the world—"Thank The Lord For Rice And Beans." When the plates came back a month or so later, she hung hers on the wall, and we ate rice and beans off of ours, meal after meal after meal.

One evening, it had been dark out for quite awhile, and although we hadn't heard a vehicle stop, someone was pounding on the door. No one ever visited us that late at night. Daddy opened the door cautiously. Brad was at the door, out of breath, and in a panic. A strange solemn sadness suddenly filled the air. Daddy listened as Brad gasped out words one after the other. Daddy grabbed his jacket and said, "I'll be back, Linda." Then they were gone, out the door. Something bad had happened.

When Daddy got back his eyes were wild with the darkest of nights reflected in them. At the first bridge below Gravel Gulch, a pickup truck had slid off the bridge, overturning in the creek. Several people were headed back to the village after a run to O'Brien Creek Lodge, the nearest store for alcohol, twenty miles past Gravel Gulch on the Taylor. Sometimes people didn't think twice—or even once—about a trip to the store when they were really thirsty for some liquor, even if was cold and stormy.

By the time Daddy and Brad got back to the wreck, the soul of Michael David had begun to cross that mysterious bridge between life and death. Daddy struggled with Brad to help lift the truck off of his body. But that night, Michael David left his wife Arlene a widow, with two little boys, ages two and three. And the village without a chief.

At night when I tried to go to sleep, my head pounded with thoughts about the little boys in the village, my daddy in the creek with the truck, and how hard he'd tried to save Michael David. Every night I prayed to God in my head over and over. Sometimes the prayers were soft and reassuring, but at other times I felt like I was just screaming quietly inside my mind to a grey cloudy sky.

The unspoken whispers of fear that had swept through the cabin finally slipped through the cracks, leaving us with winter routine. The temperature started to drop below zero, and the snow started piling up on the windows. When the wind blew through holes in the moss chinking between the logs, Mama would head out with a squirt bottle full of water to spray on the outside walls. The water would quickly freeze, filling the holes with ice. Anything to keep the heat inside the cabin.

Daddy spent many of his days out in the woods, hoping to trap marten for fur to sell. But he wouldn't hurt the one little female that hung around the yard. He treated her like a pet, sometimes leaving fish out for her at night. At first, she was timid and kept her distance, but after awhile she got brave enough to eat right out of his hand. Daddy had always killed marten for their fur so we could have money for food and light, but this one had crept into his heart by simply being nearby and hungry. So he fed her instead of turning her into cash for food.

Those creatures who wandered close by the house often became an extension of our nuclear family of five. We grew accustomed to seeing the bold little marten and chattering squirrels in the gulch. After they grew less wary of us, we learned how to mingle together. We laughed because of their animal antics and felt glad that they trusted us as companions in a mutual world.

John Charles, Sara, and I were the only kids all the way to Eagle. We all missed having the Patricks down the road. Months passed. Only adults stopped by every few weeks at most to check in on us, give us mail, or something fresh to eat. So squirrels and marten were a welcome social life.

Then something unbelievable happened. I was invited to Eagle for Andrew Kozarik's birthday party! Richard Kozarik had driven his snowmobile out to Gravel Gulch to visit and verbally deliver the invitation. "Andrew sure would like Eartha to come to his party. I could drive her in for it and bring her back later the same day."

"Well, we'll have to wait and see what the weather brings. But if you wanna come get her, I guess she can go."

Andrew was one of my best friends in town. Since Daddy had worked for Richard some before we went back to Georgia, I was able to get to know him and his two little brothers, John Paul and David. Andrew was just my age. He knew a lot of things that you couldn't get from books. Like how to blow bubbles with bubble gum. And how to ride a bike.

For days before the party, I was sick inside that I might not be able to go even though Daddy had said yes. There was no way of knowing what the weather would say. I squirmed inside. I distracted myself with schoolwork. I scratched at my skin where it itched until it bled. I prayed.

When Andrew's birthday came, the temperature was right at 20° F. Perfect weather. I was glad Andrew had a dad who would drive forty-eight miles in one day on a snowmachine in below freezing weather to get a kid to a party.

It took all day. I started out riding on the back of a snowmachine for twelve miles safe from the wind behind Richard Kozarik. What a thrill it is to ride those machines when the temperature is not too cold and you have on just the right amount of clothes!

When we got to Andrew's house—the one I was so jealous of because it was such a fancy box house compared to our crumbly cabin and so close to town—Terry Kozarik showed me around to see who was there. I wanted to have Andrew all to myself, but it was his birthday, and so I knew I would only get to spend a little time with him while I was there. His little brother ran around sucking his thumb, and I thought maybe he'd be fun to talk to, but I watched him for over fifteen minutes, and the thumb was not leaving its home. Soon the spotlight was on Andrew as he opened his presents, and everyone scrambled to see what he now owned. Afterwards I ate cake and ice cream together with kids who were no longer strangers. And then, finally, the snowmachine ride back home. Home to the shelf-bed to sleep where images of children danced in my head for a long time before I fell into sleep. How many hours had I been gone?

John Charles was dubbed the official timekeeper. He could tell us what the numbers were on his watch, but that didn't mean they would match the time in Eagle. It just meant that we could have a dependable Gravel Gulch time zone to go by. The only alarm clock we used was Daddy's internal one, which normally went off at about 6:00 in the morning. Unless it didn't. Daddy—still lazing in bed—often yelled at John Charles.

In the Bush, where mostly wild animals live in and among the trees, life floated by, along with time. John Charles had a watch that was usually within an hour or two of the time zone in Gravel Gulch, but the day began when Daddy's internal alarm clock went off. "John Charles! Get up. Build a fire. Make the coffee." John Charles didn't even drink coffee. For all Daddy knew, it was only three o'clock in the morning. Sometimes the room could stay a bitter biting cold for over an hour before the fire would warm the house enough for the frost around the windows to begin to melt.

One of my usual chores was to grind wheat for Mama to make into bread and gravy. Chuck and Peggy had given us bags of old wheat berries that they didn't want to take back with them to Georgia. They had gotten them for free by cleaning grain bins on their way to Alaska.

The first step of the job was to go through the wheat berries and pick out any little rocks or dead grasshoppers. It was tedious work, making sure the tiny kernels were clean enough to be ground. Then I would put handfuls of the berries in the mouth of the grinder, but not too many, or I wouldn't have the strength to break them. As I ground the berries, the light brown powder fell into the pan in two little mountains that had to be knocked down to make more room for more mountains to form. Over and over, I worked the handfuls through the grinder to make flour.

Mama had another grinder, a smaller one that was used to make "hamburger" meat out of whatever large game was available. Mama almost always ground the meat, which just squished through the grinder as the gears turned, red and bloody.

We always had something to eat, even if it was basic and dull. Once we dwindled down to a box of frozen turnips on the front porch, a three-pound bag of barley, and an old can of bacon grease that us kids had dug out of the storage cache down below the cabin left behind from decades past. Mama boiled some barley with turnips for soup while Daddy walked to town with furs that he had tanned from marten to sell. It was −40° F, but one of our friends with a snowmachine would surely bring him back with some food, coffee, and fresh tobacco before too long.

Daddy and Mama didn't mind eating anything as far as I could tell. John Charles and Sara didn't always care for what was on the table—but I had always been the pickiest by far. Mama had a question for me one day that made me think for a very long time. "Do you know how to tell if you're rich or poor?" It was a hard one. I thought maybe it had something to do with having running water, or electricity, or a snowmachine, but she answered, almost to herself, "Whether you worry more about starving to death or getting fat."

Even though us kids had grown like weeds over the summer, Daddy and Mama always stayed about the same size. Average. So I figured we were somewhere near middle-class.

We certainly weren't cursed with the hunger you see in magazines where flies are buzzing all around bodies lying about with vacant eyes, but we didn't *ever* throw food away if it was salvageable at all. If a block of cheese starting turning green, we just cut the green off and finished eating the yellow.

I knew how hungry I had to be before I would eat some things. Even though we had breakfast, lunch, and supper every day, I stayed desperately thin. Mama just said I was a picky eater. I loved squirrels, rabbits, grouse, and could even handle fish day after day. But moose, caribou, and bear were a struggle. I didn't like to gnaw on some chunk of meat full of gristle until I could swallow it. I'd eat just enough to stave off my hunger.

And no matter what, I couldn't eat mushroom soup. I just couldn't. When Mama made it, all I wanted was a biscuit, but she still made me take a bowl for my place at the table. I would sit there and take a few spoonfuls of the evaporated milk broth off the top. I could handle that. But not the soup. Mama threatened to put it away for my supper, but I wasn't going to touch it. I would be hungry until she let me starve. I knew I could be more stubborn than her on that account if it was going to involve day old mushroom soup.

On one of the days when Mom had made the gruesome soup for lunch, Sara was eating away. "I'd rather eat this soup than get bit by a big ole dog." She didn't hate it like I did.

I said, "Not me. I'd rather get bit by a dog." I sat there and chewed on my biscuit.

CHAPTER TEN

"Life Isn't Fair"

DADDY JUST DIDN'T buy new clothes. I wore hand-me-downs from other kids my size, and Sara wore my hand-me-downs and others from kids her size. And sizes were flexible. We all wore things that people had gotten tired of and decided to give to us rather than throw them away. And the ones they did toss we could always look for in one of our treasure hunts at the local dump. Daddy wasn't one to mail order us the latest outfits, but we still had plenty of clothes. Sometimes it took a lot of layers just to stay alive.

As Sara got potty-trained, Mama didn't have to work near as hard on laundry. Sara still wore cloth diapers at night, but during the day she was using the size number ten coffee can that was my little toilet. It was only able to hold three quarts, a much better fit for us girls instead of the big five-gallon bucket that Mama and Daddy had for themselves.

Mama was always behind on laundry during the winter. She sometimes wore her jeans for weeks upon end. Dirty clothes sat in a huge pile on the front porch, waiting for a warmer day, and then when a warmer day did come, there often seemed to be so many other chores that needed to be done first. When she managed to wash clothes, she would hang them out on the line. She tried to shake the wrinkles out, but before she could they were already frozen into the clothing. She had to work fast, hanging them up quickly, so that the ones on the bottom of the pan wouldn't be frozen solid by the time she got down to them. My clothes, baby clothes, underwear and socks were first priority.

John Charles and I were busy with school, but not as busy as kids who were in public school. We worked at our own pace. Usually we spent about four good hours a day on schoolwork. Sara was now enrolled in Head Start, a program that operated out of town. Her instructor, JoAnn Millie, came out by snowmobile once every month or so to give Sara toys that would help her learn. At Gravel Gulch, we were all in school in our own way, constantly being challenged by our environment. Nothing changed the fact that the cabin was small. As me, John Charles, and Sara kept growing, our world was more and more crowded. Even the logs of the cabin felt the weight of gravity. Over the years the lower ones gradually kept sinking, valuable inch by valuable inch into the ground. We didn't have to look up very far to see the ceiling.

Sometimes the lessons were harsh, cruel, haunting beyond measure. Cabin fever brought out the worst in everyone over time. Isolation from the rest of the world inevitably took its toll. Yet, after a quiet snowfall, with a light glow from lamps softly glimmering, all could be hidden, tucked away into a wilderness that only some can dream about visiting.

Sara had night terrors from time to time. When she did, she woke us all up, screaming, "Mama, Mama! There's snakes in my bed! There's snakes in my bed!" At first, Mama would get up and go sit beside her, carefully going through Sara's blankets to assure her that nothing was there.

I always knew what would happen next. Sara didn't understand that snakes didn't live in Alaska. I had told her over and over that snakes couldn't live in Alaska because it was too cold, but still she screamed that there were snakes in her bed. Her screams shook the air. She wouldn't be quiet. When Daddy snapped, he started screaming at her to stop screaming. She couldn't turn herself off, so Daddy would decide to flip the switch himself. He'd get up out of bed, mad as hell, reaching for his belt. After he cracked it across her back a few good whacks, the snakes of her dream would finally die, and her screams would turn into whispery yelps.

I didn't dare move a muscle except to breathe. I lay frozen on my beloved shelf-bed that had been added to the wall long before we had moved there and waited for it to be over. There was nothing else to do.

If only us kids could get away, even for a few hours a day . . . .

What Daddy said went. And that was that.

Maybe I could win the Ranger Rick story contest, if only I put the exact right words on paper. All the winners got to go to a camp for two weeks in North Carolina. I knew Grandma and Grandpa would drive to see me. Every year, I had another chance, another story to send away.

Daddy made almost all the rules. Or the Bible. Sometimes he let Mama make them, like with school assignments. And Michael Buck insisted on us following his guidelines for sending in our work. But Daddy made sure that we lived where he was the one in charge. No social worker, police, doctor, lawyer, or Indian chief was gonna tell him what to do. Or the rest of us for that matter.

Still, slivers from other worlds slipped through the cracks of his rigid structure. Visitors, summer trips into town, schoolbooks, storybooks, and our own understandings of God's Holy Book all carved their own invisible markings on our souls that could not be caged. No matter how hard Daddy tried.

Daddy didn't do as good without weed. If he ran out of herb in the middle of winter, you had better behave. He would search every corner high and low until he knew all his stashes were gone. He even swept the dust from underneath the bed, hoping to find enough to help him get to a different place. He would go outside and look through the dirt that was all mixed with snow that had already been thrown outside.

When he was out of weed, any little thing irritated him. He raged about the simplest offenses. Then I was constantly cautious, but reckless little Sara had a talent for committing trivial crimes at the wrong time.

Earlier, before I had started having real schoolwork, I got mad at Michael Buck because he wouldn't send me coloring books. So what if they hampered creativity. I didn't want to draw my own. If I had a coloring book, I could sit and color mindlessly. My surroundings would fade into a backdrop. I wouldn't have to invent or create anything in the process. All I wanted to do was stay in the lines, lines that I hadn't already drawn myself.

"Life isn't fair," I pouted during one of his visits.

He responded, "No one ever said it was going to be fair, Eartha."

But when I started to get more and more things in the mail, the misfortunes of my life seemed to balance out a bit. Michael Buck kept subscribing to magazines for my brother, and now me! Ranger Rick, Highlights for Children, Zoo Books, Cricket, Boy's Life, National Geographic World, Weekly Reader, Electric Company, Sesame Street, Jack and Jill, Ladybug. I got new issues almost every time someone came out with the mail. Sometimes John Borg brought the mail out on his snowmobile or somebody out running their sled dogs might stop in with a few weeks' worth.

The brand new magazines brought life to the dim room of Gravel Gulch. Even Oscar the Grouch who lived in a garbage can seemed pretty happy about it. Pictures of ostriches and snails, stories about children from all over the world, drawings, instructions for crafts were right at my fingertips.

December brought not only Christmas, but also the Solstice. Four hours of grey twilight during midday would slowly turn into five and then to six. Even though it was dreadfully slow, at least we were up on the downhill slope towards the midnight sun.

Sometimes, you could almost believe that life was fair at Christmas time. The taste of a sweet mandarin orange that someone brought out couldn't last forever, but it sure stayed on the tongue for awhile.

We had a little spruce tree standing near John Charles' bed, but spruce just didn't smell near as much like Christmas as the pine in Georgia. And the needles all pointed in the wrong direction so any ornaments that we made had to be put on extra-good so they wouldn't fall off.

Some of our goldminer friends who we had met the summer before at American Creek Campground surprised us when they sent a new batch of hand-me-downs out for me and Sara. A package came from old friends from the South carrying the familiar smells and tastes of the past—pepper relish, muscadine jelly, corn, chestnuts, peanuts, and pine branches. And we always counted on Grandma and Grandpa to send a big package of wonder. As we dug through the box after Mama read the letter, we found boxes of Jell-O, a magical powder that changed form if you put it in water and got it cold.

"Mama, can we make some soon? Pleeease?   Pretty please?" Sara and I begged.

It didn't do any good to follow the directions on the box since we didn't have a refrigerator. We couldn't put it outside because the temperature was too cold. It would just freeze solid instead of jelling like the box said. You were supposed to have to wait four hours after mixing it all together for it to be ready but that kind of math didn't work at all. Four hours was a heck of a long time.

"Well, I don't see why not. We'll just put it on the floor. It's good and cold there," Mama said. It was ready in about an hour. The first couple of feet off the floor never really got warm when it was cold outside, even when the cabin was warm everywhere else. On the bottom shelf of the cupboard reconstituted milk formed ice crystals as we walked around the room wearing T-shirts.

Michael Buck brought Mama and John Charles a guitar for the holidays. The only music we ever got to listen to was on "Caribou Clatter". John Charles started practicing chords from the book that came with it when the weather was extracold. It only took G, C, and D for him to be able to put together a tune that sounded mighty fine.

Mama sometimes picked it up and started strumming right along. She had been taught how to play the piano while just a kid. "My mama wanted to take lessons when she was a little girl so bad she couldn't stand it, but nobody had the money for them. So she made sure I learned." Mama half-complained. But the other half was busy being glad she knew some about music. Before long, she was playing the guitar.

"Will you play a song, Mama? It'll help me sleep," I often pleaded after I climbed onto my shelf-bed for the night. If you got her started, she didn't usually stop at just one. She often sang reassuring gospel lyrics or Kris Kristofferson tunes as her fingers danced away on the strings in the dim light of the room.

"Mama, will you stop?" Sara didn't like it at all.

"Play just one more. Just one. Pleease, Mama, please?" I didn't care what Sara thought.

Every night before bedtime, Mama held Sara on her lap with the Bible in her hand. I sat to one side of her, John Charles to the other. Daddy lay on the bed. The cabin suddenly got very quiet, a moment of silence. Mama picked out a chapter from the Bible to read, and we all listened at her soft voice as she brought the still words to life. Those evenings, when the wind maddeningly blew around the four tight walls of Gravel Gulch, and the temperature dropped to –40° F or –50° F or –60° F, Mama's comforting voice and the words from the Bible became a refuge on an island that had no sea.

The sun was slowly coming back on the distant mountains but still much too far away from the valley. Mixed with love for the sight of long-missed golden colors and the pale blue of winter sky was the tiresome cold that clear weather often brought along.

On one –30° F day, John Charles stayed out almost all day, chopping up wood ahead in case the temperature dropped even more. He was recovering from a cold, and every time he would come in the house to warm up, his nose would start dripping.

"It's time to go back out, my snot's thawing out."

I stopped asking, "What's the temperature?" Instead, I would ask, "What's the below?"

For Brad down the road, the world was a completely different story. In the middle of one of the cold spells—on a rare warm day when the temperature was above zero—he decided to pay a visit to the Hinkley family. They lived across American Summit, several miles farther out the road than Gravel Gulch. Daddy agreed to drive him out on a snowmobile that Richard Kozarik had lent us to use for awhile, but after a few miles, Daddy didn't think he would be able to make it to the Hinkleys because of drifting snow. He offered to take Brad back to the mine cabin, but Brad decided to take off walking with several miles to go before he reached the family's home.

Later, we heard that Brad made it to the Hinkleys by evening where he spent the night. When morning came, he took off walking for Dawson City, Canada – more than 100 miles away. He wore a pair of jeans and some thin rubber boots. A few days later, when the temperature dropped to –45° F, he may have already walked across the border, slipping through Dawson without a trace. Or perhaps his dark raven skin has since blended with the soil of the Earth as his spirit rests in a place some call Heaven.

Back in the valley, winter continued its mad descent towards an inevitable spring. Before the road crew started coming through on the snowplow, Daddy made a trip into Eagle to return the snowmobile he had borrowed from Richard. Someone would be sure to give him a ride back to our cabin, but it was time to think ahead. Snowmobile weather was slowly dwindling to a close. Daddy took the battery for the '57 Chevy along because it had to be recharged before the van could start. He also bought a new set of spark plugs, our ticket into town when the road opened.

Soon after the snowplow cleared the road, patches of gravel began to appear. We took long walks then, scraping our boots over the stones again and again just to feel the ground. Some days when we were out, the plow would pass by, pushing away yet another layer of winter.

This time, the yellow machine-creature was right behind us, moving in fast.

"Mama, hold me! Hold me!" I screamed, panicking. Mama already had about thirty pounds of Sara bearing down on one hip. She wasn't about to pick up a six-year-old kid that wouldn't shut up just so they'd be quiet.

"John Charles, will you hold me? Pleeease?" I was beyond desperate.

He just laughed.

I wasn't sure if the driver was the type to plow little girls into the snowbanks as he did his job. All I knew was that gigantic dinosaur was doing its thing, and I was in the way. I glanced back and saw the snow as it piled into great berms on the sides of the road. I imagined being buried alive. Mama and John Charles would be so sorry.

I panicked again, and then bolted, running as fast as my legs would carry my body, all the way up the road to the trail that led down to the gulch. When I reached the trail, I rolled over and over down the hill until I got to the footbridge that went across the creek below the cabin.

When we first went into town, it could have been any day of the week. Daddy certainly wasn't going to be picky about it being a Friday. And if it was a school day, well, that was one of the trade-offs of correspondence. You couldn't earn perfect attendance. It wasn't part of the program.

I was old enough now to know exactly where we were going. For sure, we would hit Helmers' General Store, the dump, the P.O., the hardware store, and the Kozariks.

At Helmers', Daddy bought bananas, two frozen pizzas, and a six-pack of Pepsi. He was ready for something different than moose, fish, oatmeal, beans, rice, biscuits. Sara and I each had a ten-dollar bill that Grandma and Grandpa had sent us at Christmas.

"Buy anything you want as long as it's food." Mama told us.

We would've started running up and down the aisles, that is, if there were any. Instead we looked up and down the rows of shelves. Ten whole dollars? That was a lot of food.

Sara had been addicted to pickles ever since she could eat. She had to get a jar of those. I was thirsty for orange juice and wanted a box of peach-colored Jell-O. Sara decided to get us all a box of cereal for breakfast some morning, and I got a can of tomato sauce so Mama could spruce up a batch of spaghetti noodles.

"I gotta have ChapStick, Mama. My lips hurt. It's only a dollar." I just wanted makeup like the little girls used in the Sears and Roebuck Catalogue.

"Okay, get a tube if you want. And Sara too."

I wanted the loudest red possible. Cherry.

A few days later, Daddy and John Charles went into town mainly for the freedom of it. They had been gone several hours and then several hours more. Dusk fell and went. By early the next morning, Mama and us girls were exhausted from worry, waiting, and lack of sleep. The State Highway vehicles were pretty much the only ones traveling the road yet.

As soon as daylight started to reveal the shapes of bushes and trees outside, Mama and I took off on foot. Sara could walk just fine, but not for miles and miles. So Mama carried her. I set my body on walk mode—that trance when your mind does nothing but think of your feet moving forward and that's all that matters. For the time being. Then the wind'll pick up for sure and your scarf will be in all the wrong places.

When we reached the mine cabin, Mama decided we needed to rest awhile.

"Mama, what do we have to eat? What do we have to eat?" I was growling like a mad tiger inside. Three miles was an awfully long way.

She pulled out a bag of raisins. Mama was smart when it came to energy food. After several handfuls of raisins, Mama decided we'd better start up walking again. Almost right away, we met a couple of workers in a State Highway truck. They gave us a ride back to Gravel Gulch, explaining that Daddy and John Charles were okay.

Every spring, sheets of ice covered the road a few miles out of town at an especially sharp bend that was fed by melting snow that crowded the flow of water in the nearby creek. The '57 Chevy had slipped on the overflow at the turn, hitting the ditch right as Daddy was rounding the curve. Daddy and John Charles were fine, but the van was good and stuck.

The driver of a State Highway truck heading to Eagle had come upon Daddy and John Charles and taken them on into town. They stayed with Loren and Carol Paulke, our old neighbors when we lived in the camp where Sara was burned.

It was 9:00 in the morning by the time Mama and us girls got back to Gravel Gulch. Then time got up to the speed that it was supposed to be, at least for kids. Daddy and John Charles were already home by mid-afternoon, with the '57 Chevy, thanks to the Highway workers for getting it back on the road.

Daddy made the next trip into Eagle by himself to help Richard Kozarik build fox cages, an odd job that he did to earn a little cash if Richard needed him. This time he got back home before any of us had started to worry. But when the engine of the '57 Chevy started to overheat, he was still miles from home. He would have to abandon the van on the side of the road.

Daddy hadn't met Dave Likens yet, but in a matter of moments, Dave drove upon the broken-down van and its weary and frustrated owner. Dave pulled over and offered Daddy a ride. He was driving right past Gravel Gulch anyway. His two young daughters rode along. They were on their way home.

When they got to Gravel Gulch, Daddy invited them over to the cabin. Dave could have some coffee before heading on out the Taylor. Dave didn't see any reason why not. He didn't have a wife waiting at home for him, and his girls might have fun with me and my sister. Ashley was a grade lower than me. Her little sister Sarah was about a year younger than my little sister Sara.

Sara and I both had straight stringy hair that was terribly tangled most of the time. We almost always dreaded Mama trying to comb it. Ashley and Sarah had been blessed with curls that seemed to just fall into place. I wanted curls such as theirs like I wanted a playground or a cat. When they visited—which was very rare—I shared my schoolbooks and tried not to be shy. I wondered where their mother was and what their little world was like in their big wilderness.

Ashley and Sarah lived way out in the Bush with just their dad off of the beaten-path, miles and miles from Gravel Gulch. After Dave finished his cup of coffee, they all got ready to leave. Dave still had to drive out the Taylor another twenty miles. There he would park his truck and get his dog team ready for the final stretch home, eight miles down the river ice of the Forty Mile River. His girls rode in the dogsled with the mail and supplies from town, while Dave mushed the team on through the night.

Soon after the road officially opened, a potential summer prospector made the trip into Eagle successfully. But just the next day, a wind blew relentlessly across the rolling mountains surrounding American Summit, forming massive drifts of snow in its wake. The road crew came to the rescue with the snow-plow and Caterpillar, and after several days, people were able to drive in and out with as much ease as one can expect on the Taylor soon after the road has opened.

The potential prospector spent one day in Eagle before chartering a plane and flying out. He left his truck full of gas in

Eagle, hoping that a driver would come along at the right time to drive it into Fairbanks. He made up his mind fast that he wasn't gonna get stuck getting rich in Eagle looking for gold.

No one here can avoid the mosquitoes of spring. Or the newcomers: the tourists who pass quickly through, the seasonal miners and other adventuresome men and women, the unfamiliar preacher looking for his sheep. And anyone could be an agent sent from the government undercover—a narc looking to bust anybody who might be breaking the law, whatever those laws were. In other words, be careful and don't share your smoke with strangers before you get to know them. An outsider might interpret the lax laws about marijuana in Alaska— especially about smoking in public places (and what defines a public place)—very differently in terms of what is and isn't actually legal.

The summer before, the National Park Service had put up a big, heavy sign welcoming people to the Eagle Recreation Area. Who was the NPS to declare Eagle City an area of recreation? By fall, someone had poured brown paint over it, rendering it illegible. Then during the winter, someone sawed off the posts. The National Park Service resolutely put it right back up, just to have someone uproot it and haul it out in the middle of the river to be taken out with the ice when the river would break. At the downtown thrift shop, a single sign boldly stated, year after year, "We Don't Do Business With NPS."

The National Park Service serves as a link between Eagle and the nearby Yukon-Charley Rivers National Preserve. Tourists and locals alike have had to learn to accept the laws that have been established to protect the interests of the preserve.

A few residents worked for the NPS, making a livelihood in an area where it can be hard to earn a dollar. But NPS also became a curse word of sorts that riddled some conversations. Bureaucracy, regulation, restrictions . . . .

Ever so often, an off-the-wall character drifts in that no one will dare tolerate. What do you say to the guy that hitchhiked into town ranting about killing babies and laying out young girls on slabs? He claimed that he was a bomb ready to explode. He laughed inappropriately.

So the State Troopers had to fly in to get him.

Spring, with or without a welcome for brave visitors, was bringing sunshine, flowers and greenery, a mud that seemed to never end, and the nonstop buzz of mosquitoes and flies waking to the world once again.

By the middle of May, all of the snow had melted in Eagle, but patches still dotted the valley where the sun had been forced away by the shadows of mountains. Water was running everywhere, streaming down the mountainsides, creating rivers of mud as it went. Deep potholes formed in the road, some over a foot deep, which later could possibly serve to slow down someone who might be driving just a little too fast.

Sara and I started making ice cakes, with the primary and only ingredient being water. We'd leave containers of water outside overnight to bake at whatever temperature the air was that particular night. In the morning, the cakes would be ready, freshly frozen blocks of ice ready for decorating with soil and stones and clay from the creek.

Grandma and Grandpa Will Be Sad To See Us Go

Sara Playing Under the Clothes Line . . . Springtime!

You Must Use This Road to Get to Gravel Gulch in Winter!

Traveling Across Canada

Our Valley in the Middle of Summer

Jack Boone's Old Hardware Store

Eagle Public Library

Daddy Hard at Work Down at the Gold Hole

From Left to Right – John Charles, Sara, and Eartha See Who Can Keep
Their Feet in the Water the Longest!

Daddy Feeding a Squirrel Wearing the Squirrel-skin Vest
Mama Made Especially For Him

Sara, Eartha, and John Charles Smile For the Camera
on a Hot Summer Day

Eartha in Front of the Clothes Line

Eagle City From the View of the Bluff

Grandpa and Grandma's Round House in Georgia

Returning Home After Being Beautified at Grandma's House

Getting Ready to Go Back to the Last Frontier with the `57 Chevy in Tow

Sara Wearing Her Favorite Mushroom Shirt

Eartha Lee

Mom and Dad with American Creek in the Background

A Long Day's Worth of Cutting Wood

Eartha Goes to the Library With Sara When It's Fifty Below Zero . . .
Only Four Blocks Away!

Mom Stands in Her Garden on the Banks of the Yukon

The Last of the Spring Yukon River Ice Headed North

The House We Lost at Public Auction

Coming Down the Taylor Highway Into Eagle

Eagle's Bluff in Summer as Viewed from Historical Eagle Village

Eagle's Bluff in Winter as Viewed from Historical Eagle Village

Eagle City Hall

The Yukon River Flowing by the Banks of the Historical Eagle Village

One of the Best Little Libraries in the World!

Graduation Day From Union County High School

CHAPTER ELEVEN

"Four Hundred and Eleven Cans!"

DADDY DECIDED HE was going to fix the roof of the cabin over the summer. He said it'd be a good idea if we weren't in it while he did. Mama gave our supposedly five-person tent a brand-new used zipper and stitched the canvas to the bottom with new thread. After our long stint of camping in incessant rain the summer before, the tent needed any help it could get. Daddy was eager to get us into our big blue home, so as soon as the tent was up, we moved everything in right away.

Every day, squirrels ran around looking for scraps of food that Mama might have forgotten to hide away. Squirrels sure had smart minds if your kitchen was outside. Heck, we even had to stop using the magnetic breadbox because they were strong enough to paw their way in for some good squirrel grub.

Some squirrels you ate for dinner and others you loved. That's the way it was in the woods. Mama was playing the guitar one day by the tent, and a squirrel came over and sat on her shoe like she was a tree full of angels.

After that, I thought I could tame a squirrel. A little patience and some scraps of food would go a long way when it came to proving love. After awhile, she was brave enough to crawl up on my legs and arms and eat whatever I held.

Then she became a mama to three babies. "She'll get mean now that she's a mother," John Charles warned. "You should stay away from her because she might bite you."

I figured John Charles knew more than I did about the whole mama squirrel thing. So I kept my distance. I even got a little paranoid. One day, I saw her coming straight at me and thought maybe she was gonna jump on me and bite my face. And then, because little girls and mama squirrels don't care too much about fighting, we both ran. At just the wrong time. I felt my foot sliding on her body as soon as I hit with my step.

I hurled myself crying through the front door. I felt sick inside.

Daddy had his own ways of proving love for a squirrel—one he didn't want to have to do this afternoon. But he picked up a stick of stove wood and gave her a good strong hit for mercy's sake.

Daddy started cutting wood to sell to his customers in town, but he knew he couldn't keep sawing down trees to raise his family without doing something more to add to his income. Early in the summer, overhead employees from the Bureau of Land Management came in from Tok to administer the yearly physical test to wildfire fighters who had already taken the required coursework.

He had to step up and down on a wooden box at a pace set by the sound of a continuous beat on a cassette tape that played nearby for the duration of five minutes without stopping. Up down. Up down. Up down. Up down. Afterwards, one of the officials from Tok took his heart rate to help them know that he was in fit condition to do the tasks related to those of a wildland firefighter. Dad's heart wasn't in the best of shape, but it passed the test! When Dad could fight fire, it was like he was working in his true career.

After sitting on its wheels all winter, the '57 Chevy wasn't squealing its tires to get back on the road. Going to town was one thing, but when a cord of wood was loaded in the back, the van became almost as cantankerous as Daddy. If Daddy ended up having to mechanic around with it, he'd start cussing away like it would solve everything. After he went through enough dirty words, he'd get to feeling bad enough to actually feel better. Then he could make some progress on fixing whatever malady had happened to the van. If it needed new parts, he'd have to fork over the cash, but he had to have it in working order to be able to haul the wood to get the money to fix it.

Early in the summer, Daddy got a visit from one of the fire-fighters in town. The BLM superiors in Tok had finally called Eagle needing a crew of sixteen qualified workers to fight a fire near Northway, about 125 miles away by air. They asked Daddy if he'd be a squad boss. Squads worked in groups of four with one firefighter acting as their leader. All four squads were under the direction of the crew boss. Daddy didn't earn as much as the crew boss, but he got a higher hourly wage than the other people in the squad.

We all went into town on the day of fire call, even though it wasn't Friday because Mama needed to drive the van back to Gravel Gulch. We waited with Daddy at the BLM building until it was time for him to board with the rest of the crew. The twin-engine plane took off on the grassy runway covered with poppies and strawberry plants growing all along the sides and headed straight towards the Yukon as it gathered enough speed to get off the ground. By the time the last drones of the plane faded away, Mama was already in over her head as far as being in charge of the household.

Mama didn't like to drive the van, but she didn't dare let John Charles behind the wheel. He was twelve, but the law said you couldn't try for your learner's permit until you were fourteen. Some laws didn't matter when it came to Daddy, but how old you had to be to drive was just shy of an eleventh commandment.

The starter in the floorboard of the van was right next to the clutch which was right next to the brake which was right next to the gas pedal. Mama's size five feet wouldn't have been able to manage getting the van a foot forward, let alone all the way home, if it weren't for the extra inch or so her shoes gave her. She had to use the heel of her left foot to push the clutch in while she pumped away on the starter with her toes. At the same time, her right foot was busy giving the van some gas, but not too much or she'd have to slam the brake right off, especially if she'd had to park on a hill.

Daddy might be gone for up to twenty-one days, the maximum time allowed without "r & r"—a three-day break for rest and relaxation. When Daddy was gone, Mama seemed kind of like an abandoned person. She didn't have the practice necessary to enforce the law around the house like Daddy preferred. He was the head of household, and without his brain around, us kids saw all kinds of forbidden possibilities. Would we *really* have to eat three square meals a day? What about five round ones? What if we got a little too loud?

One night everything got mixed up. Benny Juneby had run in the ditch less than a mile up the road. He showed up with his wife and baby boy at Gravel Gulch thinking Daddy would be home.

"Georgia! Georgia!" That's what he liked to call Daddy.

Mama walked outside and looked up at the top of the trail where Benny was standing by the road. It was two-thirty in the morning, but the sun was hardly setting at all anymore. Just a poke down and then right back up kind of sun. And even when it was down, the world still stayed bright enough to see by. She decided we'd take them back home to the village.

It didn't look right to see Mama driving the '57 Chevy. But she did it okay, making it to Benny's without having to deal with any crazy van tantrums. After dropping Benny off in the village, Mama caught town fever on the way back through Eagle. So we went to the dump to find buried treasure, and then on to explore the little garden that was part ours, finding fresh lettuce in the broad daylight of three o'clock in the morning.

And we all safely made it back to Gravel Gulch, the van behaving the whole way. We hadn't seen anybody at all in town, no one else out galavanting around outside. We bantered through the town, in a secret conversation that only we heard. That night, Eagle made me think of how still life can get, even in the midst of a town or a city, so that it nearly appears absent, hidden from view like the white ptarmigan of winter against the snow.

Mama said we were blessed. She didn't ever use a gun. We were a family of hunter-gatherers. Daddy and John Charles hunted. Mama and us girls gathered. When we were foraging in the bushes picking berries or herbs for tea, we'd sing, "She'll be comin' round the mountain, she'll be comin' round the mountain," until I didn't think she was ever gonna be comin' round no mountain. But Mama had us sing and wear tinkling bells to scare away bears. She taught us that bears did not like to be surprised.

With Daddy gone, Mama decided it would be sensible for us to sleep in the cabin at night. The windows, just plastic, were plenty big enough for a bear to get through if it was in the mood. But strong, sturdy walls felt pretty safe compared to the big blue canvas tent standing on nothing but poles.

Then we ran across grizzly tracks one day when we were out walking in the woods nearby.

"Mama, what's the best way to deal with a bear if it's attacking you?" I wanted to plan ahead the best I could.

"Climb a tree, play dead, make noise, confidently walk backwards. Do not ever, ever, ever run. They will run faster than you. It's been proven." She rattled off a list.

Sara and I decided that knowing how to play dead could be essential to our survival. We took turns. She would be the one playing dead, and I would be the bear, assaulting her with love until she had to resurrect herself. Then she'd return the favor, becoming the bear while I was curled up tight on the ground.

John Charles explained, "Everybody dies sometimes, and it could happen anytime. You might live to be old or might not, 'cause a tree might fall on you."

I said, "That's not dying, that's getting killed."

Daddy got back home in thirteen days. He was all beat up, with a broken nose, tired to the bone. Glad that it hadn't been twenty-one days. His paycheck arrived just in time for winter. Aside from the usual supplies, he had his eyes set on a washing machine that Sara's old Head Start teacher had put up for sale for a hundred dollars.

The washing machine was operated entirely by hand. A main trough sat on four skinny legs with a handle on the front, attached to a chunk of metal the length of the tub. When the handle was pushed back and forth, the clothes got a good proper spin.

A load took thirty minutes in all, fifteen for the wash and fifteen for the rinse. The faster the better. Good exercise for upper arm muscles, and lots of time to think about how good it feels to do certain chores. Good-bye to the washboard and the little metal tub full of dirty clothes . . . !

The wringer that was built on the back sealed the deal for Dad. "Mama, this machine sure makes a joyful noise!" I told her as I pushed the handle back and forth, the laundry sloshing around. We were done with washboard scrubbing. And nobody had to hand squeeze the water out of the clothes once they were finished, just put them through the wringer on the machine and hang them out to dry.

For days after Daddy bought the washing machine, Mama put laundry pretty high up on the list of chores. Stacks and stacks of dirty clothes had accumulated over the past winter. Piles of them crowded the front porch to the point that there wasn't a front porch anymore.

Sara was still just four. She was jealous of the washing machine, and not afraid to get political about it. Sara stood pouting in front of Mama, in her splayed out stubborn stance, begging Mama to help her with a project. Mama wasn't about to give up her extra time when she was using it for a task as necessary as laundry.

"I think we ought to just take that old washing machine right back to Millies, that's what I think we ought to do." Sara's vote was out in the open.

We were practically upscale. Daddy had worked close to two weeks on the fire. Even now, he was earning good money cutting wood to sell to his customers by the cord.

For the first time, people who had been residents of the State for the entire previous year were able to apply for what is known as the Alaska Permanent Fund Dividend. To qualify, a person must meet specific residency standards as required by the law in order to receive a check. Our dividends, income generated by the State's surplus oil revenues, added up to five grand in all—$1,000 each, even down to Sara.

On one of our final Friday trips into Eagle for the year, we lucked out at the dump, or as Mama said it, we were blessed. At first, we were all involved in our own typical ritual in that world where one person's trash could be another person's treasure. Mama ripped apart fresh bag after fresh bag, quickly and thoroughly. Daddy wandered around kicking things aside, picking up a thing here or there to see if it was something he could ever use in the future. I looked for the particularly clean ones, translucent ones that I could examine carefully for any clues that might give a good find away. John Charles avoided being associated with the dump fun for the most part—whether or not it was helping keep an eye on Sara, exploring the woods nearby, or just hiding in the van.

While we were there, a man drove up with a whole truck full of cases of food in tin cans. He immediately began to throw the boxes onto piles of garbage.

"What's wrong with that there food?" Daddy asked him.

"Well, it all got frozen last year over the winter when I was back in the Lower 48. I don't see that it's any good now." He replied.

We started loading the very same boxes of food into the '57 Chevy. And Daddy said, "Why don't we just put those in my van here and save us a step?"

Tin cans of food rendered inedible because of having survived freezing temperatures? Well, everybody's entitled to their own opinion. In the winter we could have canned vegetables, soups, peaches, pears, fruit cocktail, ravioli, corned beef hash, potatoes. And sweet yellow corn. Later on, we would learn that canned potatoes didn't resurrect so well after being frozen, but they sure didn't require the fine-tuned skills involved in choking down food like moose gristle or soup with the dead bodies of shaggymane mushrooms floating all around under the broth of evaporated milk.

When we got back to Gravel Gulch, we started carrying the cases of food down the long trail and across the bridge—be safe, hold steady, don't fall!—and then up the short steep trail that led to the door of the cabin. Trip after trip after trip.

I dropped a whole box of corn in my wild hurry to help. Cans rolled off the trail, landing in the Labrador tea bushes and caribou lichen, but no one got angry. Daddy and Mama didn't even seem to notice. They were busy talking with some people that had followed us out to Gravel Gulch. All I could figure out was that Jehovah was just another name for God, and that our visitors were there to witness the miracle of salvation and our amazing dump expedition.

Many hands make light work, and going up and down that hill time after time again, the extra feet of a few people made the job all the easier, even if they couldn't seem to get God's name quite right. Daddy made a silent deal with them, help us out, and we'll listen to your stories about saving the world.

They looked around Gravel Gulch like it was a museum or an arboretum.

"What kind of tree is that you have there?" One of the witnesses was looking over at Daddy curiously, then back to a tall handsome female of a healthy budding marijuana plant.

The best escape was to pretend, momentarily, that adults should be seen and not heard. But after they had walked their final trek up the hill to the Taylor, leaving the valley and us behind, we indulged in a good family laugh.

We had to find somewhere to put our new grocery store. Gravel Gulch just got smaller and smaller as we got bigger and bigger, and the more stuff we put in it, the more it shrunk. It was just one room with five people, and three of us were still growing. At least nobody was in diapers now.

The best place was under Mama and Daddy's bed in between two sheets of plywood. I counted them as we lined them up in rows. "Four hundred and eleven cans!" I shouted triumphantly. When we wanted a can all we had to do was move everything off of the bed, lift up the top board, and pick out what we wanted. Every day we could have something to add to the usual fish, beans, rice, oats, moose, and bread.

CHAPTER TWELVE

"The Last of the Valley"

THE GIFT OF education arrived once again from the Alaska Gateway Correspondence School, boxes and boxes of instructional material for the upcoming school year. When my second grade kit and John Charles' seventh grade came in the mail at the end of August, we began our studies right away.

Things began to fall into place at Gravel Gulch a little better than in years before, even though we were quickly progressing towards the stark winter of the deep wilderness. Mama was able to work on projects without constantly being preoccupied with a baby and that old interminable task of laundry. The washing machine fit fine in the cabin for doing laundry, so Mama dragged it in off of the front porch when she decided to do a few loads.

At Gravel Gulch, when Mama skinned a squirrel for dinner, she wasn't thinking about a plastic wrapper that could just be thrown in the trash. She had decided a long time ago that she needed a project that used squirrel furs. Now she had a whole collection of tanned hides and moreover, a little time to do something with them.

She decided that she was going to make Daddy a vest. When she had finally finished, she said, "I'm gonna write a book called 'How I Made My Husband a Squirrel Skin Vest in Only 9,998 Hours'." But my mother was raising kids in the valley, not writing books, so she put the joke aside and told me to stand on a couple of pieces of paper real still.

It tickled when she drew around my feet, but I struggled not to move. If I wiggled my feet around, she wouldn't be able to get the right size.

"You need a good pair of mukluks," she said.

The Athabaskans had perfected the art of designing mukluks, a tradition that had thus far withstood the brutal hurricane of an inevitable impending outside culture. Mama made mine using a pattern from ages ago, passed down to her from elders in the village. She freely made changes as needed: deerskin from Georgia substituted for caribou hide, heavy leather that was once a briefcase became the soles. But the end result was the same. When the temperature dropped dreadfully cold, mukluks could keep feet warmer than boots, especially with a good set of liners and two or three pairs of wool socks, but you didn't dare wear them when the temperature was above freezing. The water would ruin them.

The harsh wind and biting cold, coupled with the dark and isolation were omnipresent forces that affected our everyday living. Sara liked to call lunch the light meal. It was the only meal we ate when it wasn't dark.

"Mama, why didn't God divide the year up different? It'd make a lot more sense if he would have given us two months of snow, then two months of sun, two months of snow, and another two of sun." I was frustrated with the current setup.

The Hinkley family still lived on the other side of American Summit. In the summer, the journey wouldn't seem all that far by vehicle, but in the winter, a mile could be as a thousand miles. Bob Hinkley, the father, had split over the summer, leaving his wife, Pat, behind with her four children and another on the way. Near the end of her pregnancy, she became dangerously ill during a cold winter spell of $-40°$ F, not counting the wind chill factor or drifting snow. When the temperature hung at $-40°$ F, a calm clear day was a godsend.

Roy had bought a snowmachine from his earnings over the summer, so he could make the thirty mile trip into Eagle in case the family ran out of groceries, fuel, or other necessities. But now, if he left with his mother sick and so close to childbirth,

Helen would be left in charge of everything. She was only twelve with three younger sisters. Bob had left without making sure the family had a winter supply of wood, so it had to be cut every day from around the cabin. But without Pat, where would any of them be? She ended up having to be airlifted out by helicopter to the hospital in Fairbanks where she could receive emergency treatment.

More than once, Daddy had said that the twelve miles from Gravel Gulch to Eagle was the longest twelve miles in the world. But we never lived farther out than that. For the Hinkleys and the Likens', those same twelve miles must have been shorter than Daddy imagined.

Now that Dave Likens knew who lived in Gravel Gulch, he stopped by a couple of times over the winter with his little girls, Ashley and Sarah. The four of us girls were starved for the company of other children, but at the same time, we were guarded and shy, not quite knowing what to say or do. We had so much in common, but in many ways our lives were as different as night and day. Ashley and Sarah lived with just their daddy. A daddy who had a heck of a lot of dogs. They used thirteen of them to get into Eagle, and five more back at home. Dave and his dogs were a team, and Ashley and Sarah his family. If he ever needed to stop and rest—even if it was –30° F— he'd pull over and set up camp. Better safe than sorry.

The best thing about having them as company was that they were girls. The Kozariks only had boys. The next best thing was that Ashley and Sarah were home schooled. She explored my books with curiosity, perhaps wondering what her next school year would bring. The same characters in my Sullivan Programmed Readers lived in hers as well—the curly yellow poodle Nip, the tabby cat Tab, young redheaded Walter with his responsible sister Ann and mischievous brother Sam. The only adults, the mysterious Roundabouts, always seemed to live around the next corner of adventure as the kids endlessly ate jam while the pets roamed around. Still I was so hungry for children. Ashley and Sarah seldom got to visit.

I loved doing the Iowa Tests of Basic Skills every year. It didn't matter if you lived in Alaska or Iowa or Nebraska or Mississippi because with the national test you could be almost anywhere. You just had to have the test and somebody to give it to you who cared about following the instructions so your results would be accurate.

Learning the results taught me that I was strong. Knowing that my scores were competing well with students who excelled all across the nation gave me self-confidence that even if I might just have squirrels for friends, I was sky high on the charts when it came to Spelling.

I wondered about that other world where I was born called Georgia. Packages and letters from Grandma and Grandpa gave hints. My mind lingered on memories of the winter we had spent there when I was five. I could go back even farther, before we ever moved to Alaska, before Sara, to a few brief moments. But they were only glimpses into a realm of vanilla ice cream, ice cold lemonade, bluegrass music in a meadow, and balloons you couldn't let go of or you'd lose them.

"Mama, is it really true that you can drive all winter in Georgia?" We hadn't had company for awhile, and I was running a high temperature because of cabin fever.

When the day almost stopped showing itself at all, time became a shadow, a dim reminder that spring would come. It kept the months moving forward, but what did an hour really matter? When the thin red line of mercury on the thermometer fell out of sight day after day, the rest of the world seemed to be suspended from our reality, like a spider hanging from its gossamer of spun silk, waiting.

The air became stale with weariness. Each long dark morning, the day felt as if it would never really happen at all. Then a brief tease of twilight toyed with us, begging us to go out of doors, even if it was dreadfully cold. If I listened hard enough, I could almost hear it say, "Perhaps today, the day will come and stay for awhile."

My textbooks and storybooks, the dictionary, Mama's cookbooks, the Bible, and my magazines all eased the passing of time that froze in space. An embroidery kit given to me at my last birthday party helped to speed up hours spent by the kerosene lamp. The harder I worked, the faster they flew. A guidebook taught me of satin stitches, slip stitches, French knots.

I struggled and battled my way with it, and I won. I conquered a just-risen sun on the outline of the cloth, fumbling my way toward perfection. I sewed flowers all underneath, and little green leaves in all sorts of places, doing just what the book said to do. I etched the backdrop of a peace symbol as instructed with a simple quick stitch in dark brown. I saved the intricate border of the piece for last, one circle within another, with a design of XXXX's in between the two. By then—so close to the end—I could dance with the needle. I knew the language.

The words were difficult. I twisted thread over thread, playing and working with the needle to create the graceful curly letters and numbers in bright shades of red, blue, green, and yellow that read "Love and Peace 4 you 4 me 4 all" in stocky bold fonts.

Games of Scrabble, hours of study, and cooking with Mama made Gravel Gulch a home in the woods. Still, the cabin would sometimes catch fever without even a warning. Then it became a cell without escape, a jail of four walls.

When the first splash of alpenglow appeared on a far mountain, the pulse of time quickened. If the day were not too cold, Mama took us up to where the sun was shining. We all hiked up the mountain in the deep snow of winter, wildly breaking through with arms and legs to stand in the gold for a moment or two. The sunshine was much too far away to be the least bit warm yet, but the weeks gathered speed as each day brought several more minutes of light, spinning and twirling like a skater on ice.

"Mama, do I have to do school?" I whined as she set the timer for yet another hour of study. It was light outside now, even this early in the morning. I could be making mud pies, picking the soft spring buds from pussy willows, or sliding on ice that had been covered with snow. But I still had to work on my fractions and sentences.

One evening when summer was still young, and we were all in bed for the night, a truck stopped behind the van up on the Taylor. Daddy went outside to see what was up. Somebody shouted down at him, "Do you want some moose?"

Daddy yelled back across the valley, "No, I don't want any." The liquor store about thirty miles out the road was getting a lot of business now that the road was open.

"Do you want some moose?" The guy yelled again.

Daddy heard him right that time. "John Charles, let's go." A dead moose out of season was like Christmas in May. When they got home it was late in the night; their clothes splattered with blood, mud, and slime from butchering the moose into sections. They were exhausted after carrying one heavy chunk after another to the truck. The moose had been shot in the woods right below the road several miles out the Taylor from Gravel Gulch.

The story of how the moose was killed was more than a bit far-fetched, but it would have to do if the Fish and Game heard about it. "Well . . . it could have been the work of a random tourist who wanted something new to write about in their journal. Who knows?" In any case, it was somebody's responsibility to clean up the mess.

For the next two weeks, we lived, breathed, and ate moose. Mama set up a processing center outside in front of the cabin right away. She worked cutting huge strips of meat into small chunks. After she gave several jars a quick bath in boiling water, she filled each one close to the top with the chunks, making sure to add a little salt for flavor.

The pressure cooker sat on a Coleman stove when it was going through its cooking process. My job was to watch the gauge on the pressure cooker. The temperature had to stay between the tenth mark and the thirteenth mark. I could read a book at the same time, but I had to pay close attention. Every time I turned a page, I looked back up at the gauge.

The flame on the propane Coleman stove constantly flickered up and down. Depending on the wind, the gauge could drop down or shoot up in a matter of minutes. When the little red needle got down to the tenth mark, I adjusted the knob on the stove to give it a bit of heat. If the extra heat caused the needle to shift over close to the thirteenth mark, I adjusted the knob so that it would cool off a little. After an hour and a half of reading in the wind and shifting the knob, the batch would be done.

Even though it was June, there were still huge shelves of ice along the creek bed. Mama turned one of them into a giant refrigerator so the rest of meat would stay fresh as the days passed. One of her friends had told her that a moose was a mighty big animal to try to fit in a quart jar, but by the time she finished, she had succeeded in putting half of a moose into 105 quart jars, except what we ate along the way.

"I think I'd rather have chicken," Sara said at lunch one day.

I wanted two presents on my eighth birthday. Not having to do dishes was a given. So was a chocolate cake. As for other presents all I wanted was a little green hatchet that Mama and Daddy had stored away for the longest time, but they had said I had to wait until I was old enough to use it. And I didn't want to have to eat moose on my birthday.

Then I found out Daddy was going to give me an even better present than I could imagine. He was headed into town to take care of errands. "I reckon you could come along." He said it like it was no big deal. I knew I never had to do dishes on my birthday, but going all the way to town with Daddy! All by myself! Mama was up to her ears in moose, so she couldn't even think about going.

When I was littler, I had tagged along behind him with a pie pan looking for gold in the creek, but it'd been forever since I'd went anywhere with just Daddy. I walked up the hill to the '57 Chevy with butterflies flying around in my stomach. Just when we got to the top, a truck full of people pulled over to the side of the road to let Dad know the news.

"It's fire call! We need you for the crew," people shouted. I watched him quickly pack his bags so they could get to the airport as soon as possible to join the rest of the firefighters. I didn't mind so much that I wasn't going to get to go to Eagle with him. It was the thought that counted—the getting ready to go, the hike up the hill to the van—the looking-forward-to-it-all part that mattered.

So Daddy flew out to fight fire, Mama canned moose, and John Charles helped me bake my cake. We used a German chocolate recipe from Mama's Hershey's cookbook and made vanilla pudding for frosting. I had buried a peanut butter jar full of Jell-O in the ice early in the day so it would be ready with the cake. But before any of us could eat anything else, Mama said we had to eat our moose. I sighed a heavy thought, looking down on my plate at the same sort of meal I ate every day.

When I opened my presents, there was the little hatchet up in the shed that I had wanted for such a long time. It was just my size. "Mama, did Daddy really say I could have the hatchet? Are you sure? Mama, can I go chop kindling right now? I've always wanted a hatchet of my very own! Can I really keep it? Is it really mine? Can I use it right now?" I ran outside and chopped kindling for a good half hour before it was time for moose and cake.

Early that August, we left Gravel Gulch for good, even though we didn't know it at the time. Daddy was in the mood to camp again. So we moved six miles down the Taylor to American Creek Campground. Although the campground was no longer considered an official place to camp, Sarge Waller still came out every week with free toilet paper for the outhouse.

One of the gold miners who had been staying there was good and ready to get back on the road to the Lower 48. He needed cash, and quick. So, after bargaining back and forth, Daddy paid $128 for a tent, 2 tarps, a Coleman stove, along with several assorted odds and ends. Since everything was already set up, we moved in and made ourselves at home.

The campground was filled with end-of-the-roaders who had decided this was the spot to crash for the few months of summer. Our neighbors lived in tents, camper tops, and vans. Tarps were spread over outdoor kitchens. Most everyone was into digging for gold in the nearby creek bed. Once in awhile, a tourist would pull in, expecting a usual campground.

"Is there another campground around here?" They asked, glancing around. The sound of a dredge down by the creek buzzed through the place. Women worked in their kitchens of air, and kids galloped by on sticks.

Daddy liked to tell them about Eagle Campground right in town. "You can't miss the signs going in. It's only fourteen dollars a night, but they'll kick you out after a couple of weeks."

In the evenings, Mama cooked big meals, inviting others to come and eat around our campfire. Two men from Georgia

camped next to us, Mike Henshaw and Larry Adams. Sometimes, they made supper for everyone, and whenever Henshaw
fixed his traditional huge pots of spicy hot chili, he made the
campground smell like a Mexican restaurant. The adults ate
bowls and bowls of it. Sara and I watched in the background,
stomachs growling.

"You ain't gonna eat any a' my chili?" He noticed us all by
ourselves. "What's the matter, you ain't hungry?"

"It's too hot! I tried it. It burns too bad," I said. We both
wanted it, but the sting wasn't worth it. Mama'd give us a biscuit later.

"Well, next time I'll make a mild batch just for y'all," he
offered.

Even for his first mild batch Henshaw got so excited with
his pepper we still couldn't eat it without our eyes watering like
we just got a spanking.

Playing in the woods behind their camp soon thereafter,
Sara and I discovered strange plants freshly poking through the
ground that we'd never seen before. We ran for Mama.
"Mama, come look! We gotta show you something! There's
these weird plants over there you need to see." Mama stopped
what she was doing to come see what we were clamoring about.

"What are those, Mama?" She'd never seen them in Alaska
either.

"Well, they look like bean plants. How would a bean plant
get here?" She wondered aloud. "Oh, it's that Henshaw. He's
been draining water off his pinto beans here, and now he's got
some growing."

Even though no one bothered to collect fees from our
unofficial campsites, we never had to worry about where we
would dig another outhouse. Near the end of every summer, a
sewage removal crew would come out to empty the one that all
of us at American Creek Campground shared, even though it
was technically illegal.

One day, the outhouse was out of toilet paper. Larry realized it only too late. He decided the next best thing was to take
off his underwear, use it, and then properly dispose of it in the
outhouse hole. All was fine and good until the big fancy rig
came to suction the hole. The crew set to work, and about

halfway through their process, everything came to an abrupt halt. Two unhappy men dismantled several tubes to get to the culprit that had clogged the operation: Larry's shorts. The entire campground reeked for days. When Larry fessed up, his face turned as red as the chili he helped Henshaw make.

We were the only ones left in the campground when a light snow started to fall. A homesickness for the South had set in, and there was talk among Mama and Daddy about going back to Georgia for the winter. But Daddy didn't want to have to enroll us in public school.

The home school kits in the Lower 48 cost a fortune. The best thing about Alaska Gateway School District was that the coursework and advisory instruction were completely free. And you couldn't get a better advisory teacher than Michael Buck.

After Mama had a good long talk with Michael Buck, he said that he would bend the rules a bit for us. Technically, students of the Alaska Gateway School District were supposed to live in Alaska. Fancy that. But Michael Buck agreed to allow us to remain enrolled in the program under one condition. And when Michael Buck was strict, he meant it. When he said no coloring books, you better not keep asking. It wouldn't do any good to beg if he set his mind to something.

"Linda, I'll let you teach them down there. It'll be good for them. But I'm telling you, this is temporary. I can't get away with doing this for years at a time. I'll give you one school year as long as you intend to come back up here next summer."

After that it was settled, and Daddy finally said the words we'd been longing to hear. "We're going to Georgia. At least for the winter. We'd better start packin' up!"

John Charles turned fourteen just days before we would be on the road. Even in spite of a year's worth of unpredictable arguments and brawls, violent rampages and screaming fits, broken dishes and bruised backsides, a cake meant the world on a birthday.

Mama racked her brain about how she was going to make a birthday cake. She usually could make do with a little camp oven or a cookstove, but now she only had the Coleman stove with its two burners. Going without a birthday cake was worse than a bruised backside from a beating that got a little out of hand. Daddy could get a temper for sure, hurl a dish across the room, or throw a screaming fit about whatever little thing, but on birthdays, the rules were different. You got cake. And presents. And you didn't ever have to wash a dish.

She finally decided to make fourteen chocolate pancakes fit for Paul Bunyan. After she stacked them one on top of the other using pudding between each layer for frosting, the creation leaned over like the tower of Pisa. But the flopping mess was as tasty as any rectangle cake she ever made. And just as special.

Soon we were packed and ready to go: camping gear, clothes, cases of moose, tires, pots, pans, toys, school kits, and all the bits and pieces of treasure we wanted to keep with us. Sara was just about to start kindergarten. The journey across America was her first field trip of the school year. She was full of questions, new ones every day, about the world.

At first she was scared of public toilets, but soon she was running around, flushing gallons and gallons of water away as Mama worked to stop her. "Mama, why do they put their outhouses inside?"

CHAPTER THIRTEEN

"A Winter Escape"

AT FIRST, WE moved into the equivalent of a barn. Grandma was horrified. We were sleeping in a building with a bunch of hay stacked in one of the corners. She cried as she said, "I know there's snakes in that there building. I don't want any of my grandkids to git bit by an old snake." The first day Grandpa brought her over to visit, she sobbed all afternoon.

The place belonged to a friend of Daddy's. Alex was a millionaire who looked as if he struggled to pay the monthly bills if you didn't know him any better. He had inherited a great fortune when his father had died in years past. It was good that Alex wasn't the gambling type like Daddy. Alex had decided to invest in precious metals with a good interest rate instead.

Alex wasn't into fixing up old buildings on his property, and he didn't care about owning a lot of stuff to make life easier like salad shooters and such. He did like to buy land, and he had almost 100 acres of it. He didn't want any strange neighbors living nearby. Ones that might want to tell him to clean up his yard. Or his manners.

We didn't stay in the snake-house for long. It didn't take long for even Daddy to want to get out of that building with countless bales of hay in the corner where no telling what was slithering. So he started asking around. One of his friends said, "Anceberry's. Check out Anceberry's place." Once Daddy had set foot on the property, he made up his mind. It'd work. The house was about a hundred years old and falling apart, and it was off a gravel lane away from the paved road. And the rent was cheap. $300 until spring and then we'd move out. And it was fine if Daddy had the power company come to turn off the electricity. As far as he was concerned, electricity was harnessed by the devil. He didn't make it sound too fun, but at Grandma and Grandpa's, electricity was the key to a whole new world.

I always wanted to go see Grandma and Grandpa. We visited with them every few days. When it was time to leave, I'd beg Mama and Daddy to let me stay all night, and once in awhile, they'd say yes. Then I could take a bath in a real bathtub with as much warm water as I wanted.

Back in Alaska, I took baths in the little round metal tub that Mama had used as a bed for me on the trip up to Alaska. At first the water would be soothing and warm while Sara and I shared the tub. But Sara was still a baby and didn't get to stay in as long as I did. After Mama took Sara out, I would soak until I began to quiver.

But at Grandma's house, right before my bedtime, Grandma filled their huge bathtub practically to the top for me. Then she added bubble bath and swished her hands real fast though the water, making a white layer of wonderfully fun foam for me to play in as I bathed. I got to stay in the tub for as long as I wanted, and if the water got cold, I could just get Grandma to add some more hot water. Afterwards, when my hair was all wet, Grandma would ask me if she could curl my hair with bobby pins. At first, I had no idea what she was talking about. She showed me how she could part little areas of my hair and roll the separate strands into tight circles and fasten the circles with bobby pins. Then all I had to do was go to sleep and wake up in the morning with curly hair!

Everywhere I turned, there were surprises. Grandma put all the dirty clothes in a machine and pushed a few buttons that made them wet and clean. Then she moved them to a different machine and pushed a few more buttons. When she took them out, they would be perfectly dry and ready to wear. Well, at least I thought they were ready to wear. Grandma had different notions. They weren't ready to wear until they were good and ironed.

At Grandma's, you never had to go outside to go to the bath-room. You just went to the toilet and flushed right afterwards so that whatever came out of your bottom would just disappear. And there was always soft toilet paper right from the store instead of ancient Harlequin romance novels or magazines that nobody wanted anymore like we used to have to use at Gravel Gulch.

Grandpa never had to carry in wood so Grandma could cook. She had an electric stove with burners that got hot by turning a knob. The oven had its own knob with numbers all around it to let her know when to put a cobbler in, or biscuits, or banana pudding. With a woodstove, the only way you knew the oven was the right temperature for baking bread or cookies or cakes was to put your thumb down, real fast and light, on the far right side of the top of the stove. If your thumb felt like it would burn if you held it there for more than a second, it was ready.

Grandma and Grandpa thought I'd like to watch television, but after they bought me brand-new coloring books, it didn't stand a chance. If the television happened to be on, I just ignored it as I splayed out on the floor, coloring away, page after page, with a fierce intent to stay in the lines.

The television was the most mysterious thing in the whole house. If you turned it off for even a few minutes, the people somehow all kept moving around in there. So then when you wanted to turn it back on, you never knew what they might be doing. Certainly not what you would expect. If I needed a break when I was reading a book, I could put a bookmark in it or fold the edge of the page down where I stopped. Later, the words would be right where they were all along.

When Grandpa and Grandma dropped me off at Ance-berry's after an overnight visit, I was often in a dress—ironed and all—with warm tights underneath and beautiful bobby-pin curls hanging around my face. Before I would even be tempted into changing into my trousers, Grandma would say, "Charles, you take a picture of them while she's that pretty." When Grandpa got the photo back, I was right there, all beautified, with the rest of my family all straggly in the backdrop.

It sure was fun getting pretty, the bath, feeling so clean, the curls, but the tights were just that. Tight. I didn't want to stay pretty forever. I had other things to do. Practice cartwheels.

Do somersaults. Swing. And you can't do any of those things in a dress.

Anceberry's was fine enough by Daddy's standards, but that didn't stop him from complaining. "The weather down here just ain't like the weather up there. This is a different kind of cold down here. I tell you, this is the coldest winter I've felt. I mean it," he said as he shook his head.

The house had multiple rooms. The central living room sat between a bedroom and the kitchen, and a little bathroom served as a closet. Half of the kitchen was really the kitchen and the other half was set aside for John Charles. Sara and I shared a big bedroom with Mama and Daddy.

The wind sometimes blew through the walls of the old house, setting in an unrelenting chill, the linoleum in the kitchen flapping back and forth in the wind. Daddy hadn't cut a winter's worth of wood either. We were not entirely prepared, but we did have our schoolbooks to keep us busy.

Daddy still said no school on Tuesdays. That was still field trip day to the Murphy Flea Market. Every Tuesday and Saturday. I had my own bartering system set up. I had birthday money from Grandma, ten dollars, and I could buy things and sell them for me just like Daddy. Except so much of the time I just fell in love with them and had to keep them anyway.

Daddy sometimes put us to work. "Eartha, I want you and Sara to be on the lookout for blue paint, green paint, whatever color paint looks like the van. I'm thinking about repaintin' it. Go on now, git outta here and see what you can find."

Every Tuesday, we did our rounds and reported back to Daddy. Finally he said, "Well, I think we done got enough paint." He poured all the different colors into a round metal tub like the one we used to take baths in and mixed them all together. "That'll do it."

Mama began covering the main body of the panel wagon with a roller. John Charles and I worked around the edges. I practiced what I had learned in the coloring books about staying in the lines, carefully making sure to keep the paint from getting on the tires and the windows.

CHAPTER FOURTEEN

"Black Forest Make Green Pocket"

TEN MONTHS AFTER leaving Alaska, we had completed yet another round trip from Eagle to Georgia and back. By the time we pulled into American Creek Campground, we had covered nearly ten thousand miles in our new improved traveling home. Dad had decided we had outgrown the van for our return trip North. A couple of months before we left, he invested in a full-sized 1962 Chevrolet school bus. Not that he was getting rid of the '57 Chevy. He was towing it behind the school bus up to Alaska. It was good storage. And we'd need the rig when we got up North for family transportation. We had grown used to living in the school bus as the weeks had passed, and it was not so hard traveling on the roads.

We drew stares all across the Lower 48 and on through Canada. As always, Dad wore his head of wild wiry hair that grew straight out instead of down. His beard was long and vee-shaped, covering his face to the point that I couldn't tell much about what he looked like except for hair. And his eyes. Those could give away a mood so fast, you would never know what hit you.

Mama often wore tidy flowing skirts with her hair pulled back away from her face. She looked pretty just about anywhere. You could see her face plain as day, and even when she was just downright tired, a night's sleep did her a world of good, and the next morning she would almost always be just like new.

John Charles didn't like his haircuts at all. Mama cut it only ever so often, chopping the ends off so it looked like she had stuck a bowl on top of his head and told him to be still. Sara's hair was usually completely tangled, and she had a semi-permanent rat's nest somewhere in there. Mama didn't dare try to comb it out too often, she had too much else to do. And then there was me, the picky eater of the family, skinnier than a rail, looking almost starved with my stick arms and legs.

Back in Georgia, Mama and Dad thought it would be a good idea to have a warning on the back bumper of the '57 Chevy. Mama carefully stenciled the words "KEEP SAFE DISTANCE" in neat block letters, and Sara and I helped paint them a bright fire engine red. The bus with the van in tow worked great driving across the long barren stretches of Kansas. But in the biggest of cities, we got stuck in traffic where it seemed like we'd never budge again, holding up little bitty cars as we ever so slowly plowed forward. When a stoplight turned green, the drivers in front of us would start hurrying up the street towards the next light. And we'd still be trying to get through the last green light by the time it had already turned red again.

I began my ninth birthday waking up in a campground in Babb, Montana. Later that day, we'd have to get through the Canadian border. After Dad said I could get a Pepsi and a candy bar with my birthday money from Grandpa and Grandma, I stopped thinking about how much I wanted a birthday cake. I'd always had a birthday cake. But a soda and a candy bar would be just as good for once. Especially if I didn't have to eat moose.

I popped open the top of the can just a fraction of the way so that I could enjoy the sweet bubbly sugar as long as possible. I had picked out a Snickers, my all-time favorite candy bar. As the miles passed by under the wheels of our mobile contraption, I began to peel off the outside layer of chocolate with my fingernails, one tiny fragment at a time, treating each individual morsel as the last bite of sugar in the world. At last, the bare skeleton of the bar remained, peanuts buried in a caramel heaven. I ate all the nuts first, saving the best for last. My mind was all wrapped up in the haze of my very own birthday when we crossed over into Canada. Little did I know then that I wouldn't see the Lower 48 again until I was sixteen.

As soon as we got back to Eagle, someone else had already claimed Gravel Gulch. Sure, you could live there for free indefinitely, but it wasn't yours to keep if you left it empty for a whole winter.

Since it was July, we set up camp back at American Creek Campground. Living out of doors wasn't so bad, now that we had a whole school bus for our family instead of just a tent and a tarp tied to some trees. John Charles decided to keep sleeping in his little tent. He needed a little more privacy than the rest of us.

I didn't spend much time in the bus unless it was raining or when it was bedtime. Then it was cozy to curl up on my sleeping spot. Mama and Dad had put two trunks one beside the other with a board on top for me to use as a bed. They slept in the rear of the bus on a double-sized mattress. Sara slept on a cot across from my bed on the other side of the bus.

We lived mostly outside. Mama spent hours in our kitchen under the tarp and cooking on an open campfire. John Charles and Dad dug holes in the sides of the creek bed, reaching into the deep crevices of bedrock, ever-searching for the vein that would be the winning lottery ticket.

I panned for gold almost every day on my own. I was determined to find my own specks of sparkling yellow treasure to show off to the grownups. But for money, I learned that I could pick wildflowers to sell through the mail to a business that specialized in herbs. Of all flowers, fireweed was the most fun. By the time the blossoms were ready to pick, the stems had grown as tall as me. The bright rose-colored petals easily slid off between my forefinger and middle finger with just a quick jerk up the plant. And on to the next. Until a whole field would be stark with bumblebees flying all around.

Once again, Dad had thought ahead when we were in Georgia, remembering how a few hickory chips could change fresh salmon into a meal fit for kings. Solid rounds of hickory were on the list of things that we had to take with us up North, and we had been able to bring even more than before considering the extra room that the bus had afforded us on our last trip back to Alaska.

"Can I chip off some hickory? Please?" I begged. I still had my hatchet from my eighth birthday.

"Go ahead. But be careful. That's pretty hard wood. And remember to make them small enough." Mama had begun to trust me with my little sharp hatchet now that I was getting older.

When sizzling fresh fillets were cooking on a grill placed over the open flame of the firepit, you could catch the scent of the hickory chips as they burned in the fire. Now at supper, salmon was oftentimes a warm delicious meal filled with flavor from a faraway South. The months of eating it cold from the jar in Gravel Gulch were over.

By the third week of August, the chill of winter was in the air. Snow fell for four days straight. Our campground neighbors, an 87-year-old woman, Jo, and her 21-year-old grandson, Steve, were living out of their car. They turned the heater on for a couple of hours each night before they settled down to go to sleep.

Dad started the engine to run the heater every few hours trying to knock the chill out of the air. Mama put scraps of carpet down on the floor and quilts over the windows. Even though they helped a little, the bus was still just one big refrigerator. I stayed under my covers reading book after book much of the day, huddled in a ball with ninety-seven, ninety-eight point something degrees flowing throughout my body.

Jo had to use a walker but that certainly didn't keep her in the car all day. Every afternoon, she walked around the campground for a little while. When she got too cold, she knew she could come and see us.

When Jo was visiting, she sat on the front seat of the bus where it was the warmest.

"Where's your mending, Linda? And don't tell me, with all those kids, you don't have none. I can't just sit here and soak up your heat." Jo demanded to help.

At last we had a touch of Indian summer. Dad had already found a cabin for us to live in over the winter in Eagle, but why move now? The snow was quickly melting away and a warm little wind strolled through the air. Sunshine fell from the sky.

A few days later, the time had arrived. We packed up camp and headed for the civilization of town. Eagle didn't have police, a hospital, a jail, or a social worker. No doctors or lawyers. Still they say you can grow up to be anything you want. And don't you forget it. That was why we took the Iowa Tests of Basic Skills every year.

Dad had grown up to be several different things. He was a beatnik of old, a crew boss, and a salesman. He loved to strike a deal. If his treasure was another man's treasure, he'd bargain till he thought he would profit. He traded a gun he didn't really need for a utility trailer he didn't ever use. Then he traded the utility trailer for seven and a half gallons of honey, sixty-five pounds of sugar, seven gallons of cooking oil, five gallons of peanut butter and several pounds of wheat berries to grind into flour.

Dad was born to trade. His mode of operandi was straightforward. "If you'll give me this, I'll give you that." If you bring in 300 pounds of whole-wheat flour for us when you head into Fairbanks, I'll clear your land for you. If you give me some good homegrown bud for the winter, I'll give you an ounce of gold I found.

Dad used money if he couldn't make a decent trade. He had to use it at the grocery store, the hardware store, and the gas station. There was always kerosene to buy. When it was dark, we had to have the lamps going. And in the summer, the Coleman camp stove ate fuel up like people addicted to super-sized meals.

Mama stayed creative. She didn't have any money, so she bartered whatever she could. She canned fish on the halves as in years past, one for us, one for them. Our new neighbor across the street wanted Mama to render bear fat for him for half of it back. She made a profit of six quarts of pure lard, with eight quarts of cracklings to boot.

"Can I have a few?" I begged ever so often.

"Here, but only a few." She said they were rich. They tasted something like rich.

Mama used them in cornbread. The crisp cracklings—nuggets leftover from the rendered bear fat—gave the bread a uniqueness ever so desired by a baker of fine order.

We had basic food supplies and wood for the winter, but the realm of money was a little farther to reach. Dad had borrowed $1,700 from Grandma and Grandpa so he could buy the bus for our trip back up North. He depended on a Texaco credit card for gasoline as we went. The only credit card he ever owned.

But you can't rent a cabin in the sticks of Alaska on a Texaco gas card. Good thing he found a cabin in town that we could live in over the winter, rent-free as long as Dad helped work to repair the floor and make the structure as livable as possible. And we had to be out before the end of spring. But that was okay. We had a whole school bus.

By fall, Dad wrote to Grandpa and Grandma asking if he could borrow money again. He figured $1,300 would pay off the credit card bill and get us through the winter. Dad hated to borrow money. He didn't like to have a loan hanging over his head.

Grandma and Grandpa sent a check soon after they got his letter, but none of the stores in town had enough money to cash it. The nearest bank was almost 200 miles away. The owners of the gas station came close, but they were $192 short. Dad needed the money, and they said he could use the rest as credit for fuel at the station.

We weren't the only ones who needed to get out of the woods. The Hinkleys were barely surviving on the other side of American Summit. Pat was desperate. Roy was doing what he could, but every season was more of a struggle, especially without Helen around to help with the younger kids.

Helen had left Alaska right after she turned fourteen, the legal age of marriage with parental consent. A thirty-ish year old man who was traveling through Eagle took one look at her and asked Pat if he could take her to the Lower 48. Pat gave permission, and for Helen the road ahead was a mirage.

Helen returned to Eagle less than two years later, divorced and alone. Even still, she was a model, faded clothes and all, with high cheekbones, a smooth complexion and a generous smile. Within the next couple of years, Helen met Kenny Drenk, an unusually thin man with a straggly pointy beard and curls covering his small head. Kenny had wandered into Eagle determined to survive alone in the Last Frontier, even though the cards were stacked against him. But now, he had Helen by his side.

Kenny had built a home for the two of them out of tarps, black plastic, and cardboard that surrounded a simple pole frame. They lived way up Telegraph Hill where a narrow road became rockier and steeper until it disappeared into a field of tall grass. Soon after they moved into their place, Helen gave birth to her first baby, a little boy who wouldn't learn to talk until long after he had learned to walk.

Over the summer, Pat had camped in a school bus with the rest of her family in the clearing right in front of Star Gulch. Before winter set in, they had moved the bus to a little spot at the bottom of Telegraph Hill, just a short ways from town out the Taylor. The road was always open that far. Life would be easier.

The Hinkleys worked to build a hogan for their winter home, a dwelling made from earth and branches and covered with mud or sod. But by the middle of November, they were still living in their school bus. One day, the temperature dropped to –30° F. The three youngest girls stayed with families in Eagle until the cold spell broke, while the others toughed it out in the bus. Roy hadn't finished school yet, but he didn't have enough time to do his lessons. He had to work on the hogan as much as he could to try to get it ready by December so they could be warmer.

Somebody told Dad about a place we could live in for the winter where he wouldn't be bothered for rent as long as we were out by summer. The people who owned it had more pressing priorities elsewhere and obviously weren't involved in being landlords of the shack. The general understanding was that they wouldn't do anything to stop us from moving in, but if we did, it was best for them not to even know about it. It was most certainly in dire need of repair, but it did have perks. It wasn't far from the center of town, and it was free.

We were tucked away at the end of Berry Street, a good three blocks from the center of the city where the Eagle Public Library stood, that magical place where sanity reigned. The cabin was a refrigerator in comparison to good old Gravel Gulch, but it sure beat living in a bus made of metal. Food on shelves a few feet above the floor froze solid when the temperature outside fell below −20° F. Jars and tins froze and thawed, refroze and thawed again, but their seals kept on sealing.

Then Mama had to keep the water jugs right by the stove so our water wouldn't freeze. Anything under the beds froze. Night after night, I slept in a fetal position, a trick learned long ago, with my hands between my legs and my head under the flap of my sleeping bag. When my breath circulated close to my body, I could warm myself from the inside out, ever so slow. Sara could keep her head under her sleeping bag buried all the way down, but I was too claustrophobic. Even when the room seemed frozen itself, I had to have a small hole for fresh air. Otherwise I couldn't sleep, no matter what.

John Charles slept in a small separate room in the backroom. If the cabin was a fridge, his room was like the freezer section turned up a little too high. And if you've ever worked in a Burger King or a McDonald's, you know what it feels like to go in the zone, the one when you need a new box of fries. Even after we all went to bed, he avoided the place. Lucky for him, the cabin had a back door. While we all dreamed away in the front room, he became a criminal, breaking the unspoken law of sneaking out at night. The one that God didn't bother to mention that day on Mount Sinai when Moses was paying attention.

But there weren't any commandments about the way water should behave—just cold hard facts. One day when John Charles was taking a bath in the little round metal tub we used, he didn't pour the water out soon enough. The next time Mama needed the tub, he turned it upside down in his room and knocked out a solid round of ice that stayed frozen in the corner of his room for over a month before it showed any signs of melting.

"Mama, can we go to the library today, please, pretty please?" I begged one chilly afternoon when it was about −50° F outside. With long johns underneath a pair of sturdy jeans underneath snow pants, and then about four layers on top—a t-shirt, long sleeved shirt, a couple of wool sweaters—with a snowsuit as a final touch, you were probably gonna be all right. Just don't forget a hat or two, your wool scarf, the pair of mittens with the warmest liners. Or your earmuffs.

Living near the library opened the doors to hundreds of new worlds for me, story after story, with each turn of the page. I joined the fashionable detective Nancy Drew in her mystery adventures, and then moved on to tramp about with the Hardy Boys as they solved daring crimes in their neighborhood. I slipped into the wardrobe that led into Narnia with Peter, Susan, Edmund, and Lucy; skipped through the Land of Oz with Dorothy and Toto; and crept in the cracks of creaky buildings with Sherlock Holmes. I visited the Bobbsey twins in their middle-class home on the shore of Lake Metoka.

Even though the public school was just a few blocks away, Dad was making sure that Mama still taught us. At least there were a few other kids in town that were home-taught on correspondence.

Lena Ulvi was the home-school genius who had her own computer. She became my best friend over the next few years. Darrel Sonnenberg, who had taken over for Michael Buck as the advisory teacher for Alaska Gateway Correspondence Study, tested the two of us for the gifted program which was designed to provide us with further instruction in our area of talent. We both qualified to take creative writing classes together under the instruction of a teacher outside of the home twice a week. Every Tuesday and Thursday, Lena would meet me at my house, and we would walk across the street to Miriam Dunbar's. She taught us the art of crafting words into limericks, haikus, sonnets, free verse poems, and short stories. She gave us the gifts of alliteration, of rhyme, and of meter.

Dad stopped smoking cigarettes for several months during the winter, and the already small cabin seemed to grow even smaller. I had learned to read his moods like a child learns to recognize letters of the alphabet and words in storybooks. From an early age, I had a basic awareness of when to speak or not to speak, when to ask or not to ask, and what tone of voice would least likely trigger his anger when his mood seemed volatile. I often forced myself to do my best to pacify my father.

Sometimes on Saturdays, I would ask, "Dad, can I please go to Lena's?" I'd try to time his mood just right, thinking if only he was still smoking cigarettes perhaps it would be easier. As I waited for his answer, my heart was quiet and nervous, and I shivered with hope and fear. I didn't want to hear him say, "No, whaddya think you are anyway, a go-go girl? Always wanting to go, go, go."

I had no idea what a go-go dancer was, but by the tone of his disapproval it was useless to argue with him. Of course I wanted to go, to get away from the stifled smoky atmosphere of that room where we lived day in and day out, that cage filled with the constant smell of marijuana and the dry tired air that hung around my bed making even breath seem a chore.

But once in awhile, the mood, the timing and the tone of voice would match like pieces in a jigsaw puzzle, falling together perfectly, and instead of the expected "no" and accompanying insult, he would venture a "Yeah, I reckon."

Immediately my heart would seem as if to leap back into my body from some far off place where it had been curled up like a forgotten ball of yarn, and I would push for a time frame, usually adding a half an hour more than I thought was probable.

"Can I stay two hours?"

"You don't need to be hangin' around there that long. Be back in an hour." Dad didn't get along with Lena's mom and dad, mostly because they didn't believe in God. He wasn't about to have anybody convince me that God was just a figment of an overactive imagination.

"One and a half?" I would sometimes ask, once again, depending on mood, timing, tone, repeating the cycle, hoping for the rare "Yeah, I reckon", expecting the habitual "no".

When Dad let me go to Lena's, I dressed as quickly as possible, walking as fast as I could. It took me between ten and fifteen minutes to walk to her house across town, and Dad counted travel time as part of the hour. The minutes ticked away like tiny birds flitting by a window. Lena played with public school kids a lot more than I did, but I seldom visited with anyone other than her. At least her parents would let her visit me for up to two hours, not factoring in the time it took for her to walk. They weren't scared to death that Lena would become Christianized overnight.

In spite of it all, I still loved Alaska. I wasn't dreaming of running away yet. I hated being at home so much of the time, but nature was always right out the door. It could be mean and vicious for days on end, but it always brought spring, without fail, and to me that was God.

With the coming of summer, we started to get ready to move back into the bus. Mama scrubbed it clean, washing all the windows on the inside and out. The things that had been stored in it over the winter had to be organized before we could live in it. By the end of May, we were back at American Creek Campground. Even though it was against the law to camp there, miners drifted in and out, some staying on for weeks at a time.

John Charles slept in the van at night. He set up a little green Army tent of Dad's for a place to keep his things and hang out when he didn't want to be outside during the day.

Dad decided he was going to design a proper bunk bed for us girls. He built two sturdy storage units into the lower bed so we would have a place to put our things. Our clothes went underneath the bed in cardboard boxes. I liked sleeping on the bottom, and Sara wanted to be way up high, so we both got our way with where we wanted to sleep.

The kitchen was set up outside, covered with a green tarp tied to several trees. Dad built a counter and set up a wood cookstove so Mama wouldn't have to fix meals on a campfire all summer.

I spent my days running up and down the creek bed, playing with Sara and a couple of other kids that lived in the campground. John Holt was along with his grandparents, Texas Bob and Sue. Even though he was closer to John Charles' age, he didn't want to spend his time down at the creek. He left the dredging up to his Grandpa Bob.

Texas Bob liked to drink in the evening when he panned down the concentrated dirt that he had collected from the carpet of his dredge from a hard day's work. The minute he ran out of a beer, I offered to go get him another cold one.

After so many drinks, he sometimes asked me, "Hey, darlin', how 'bout sittin' next to me and keepin' me company while I finish up this here bucket?" I moved closer, peeking into his pan as he twirled the concentrate around, hoping to see a flake or two fall into the tub of muddied water. I was better at gold panning than most anybody I knew, but because I didn't have equipment or muscle power to move dirt around, I had to get by with a pan, a spoon, and if I was lucky, somebody might have a crowbar I could borrow for a day or two.

The best bet was to pan through the tailings any of the miners had finished the night before. No matter how hard I tried to find the right place, I had trouble finding anything in the dirt and silt along the banks of the creek. Maybe a flake or two, but mostly just a sprinkle of gold dust here and there. I always had the best luck with Texas Bob's tailings. He even lost little nuggets when he was paying attention. I had a little glass pennyweight bottle where I put all my gold, hoping to get it full by the end of summer. I wanted to buy a used sluice box when mining season ended so I would be ready for the next season and be able to make my own concentrate instead of having to pan through tailings. And according to my math at what gold was selling for, a pennyweight would be plenty to get a decent sluice box.

Sara and I had grand fun torturing Texas Bob's grandson. John Holt acted like he was the biggest thing in the world because he had a motorcycle back home, and he could drink if he wanted to without anyone's permission. He might have been from the biggest state in the Lower 48 and twice our size, but Sara and I knew how to chase him down trails that we had memorized like Bible verses—until he hit a dead end—and then we'd both jump on him and bite the hell out of him.

I couldn't attack him all the time though because I wanted him to hang out with me . So I'd make bets like he couldn't get across the creek without getting wet. The creek was shallow and rocks poked up all over the place. I had already mastered stepping on stones to stay dry. So I picked the hardest places for him to cross. If he lost, he owed me a Pepsi. I almost got a six-pack from him over the summer. I was rich.

John Charles spent his days working at Harold Nevers' gold mine three miles farther out the Taylor. Harold paid him eight dollars an hour to be a raker. John Charles had to sort any big rocks and chunks of gravel away from the dirt as it was funneled through a dredge and a sluice box.

On most days, John Charles worked for ten and a half hours at the mine. When he would have to take a day off because a piece of equipment was under repair, he didn't just sit around the camp if someone in Eagle would hire him for the day. John Charles had plenty of strength and did his best to make sure that whoever was paying him was getting their money's worth. He was earning cash fast.

Before the summer was over, Dad was able to work on a wildfire near Fort Yukon, a town downriver. By now, he had climbed up the career ladder, and was able to be a crew boss for a team of 16 firefighters. He was getting paid quite a bit more than he had before. In just a few days, Dad could earn enough money to support us through the winter.

Many people on the crew lived in the village. They coined a phrase about their job. "Black forest make green pocket." After a week of black forest with a check soon to come in the mail, the crew returned completely exhausted, physically and mentally drained.

The crew hadn't been supplied with sleeping bags, mosquito nets, or mosquito repellent for their first night out on the job. They slept (or tried to sleep) on the ground, in a rainfall, assaulted alive by unrelenting attacks of mosquitoes that did not let up all night.

A new school in Eagle was being built over the summer, and Dad had applied early for a job, hoping to get work right away so he could stay at home instead of fighting fire. Although the public school down by the end of the village was still a strong sturdy building with separate classrooms and a playground, it had finally lost its cultural value.

The town theorized that a more modern building and location would be able to serve both communities better. Village kids would now have to ride the bus into Eagle. Thus the old school was abandoned, locked up, and vandalized in anger and retaliation until it was eventually torn down by the authorities.

Soon after Dad got home from the fire, he reapplied until they finally hired him to dig ditches. "They always tol' me I'd be diggin' ditches for a livin,' but they didn't tell me I'd be gettin' paid this much." After he proved himself to be a dedicated ditch-digger, he was soon putting up insulation and vapor barriers. By the time the school was finished, he had earned a few good paychecks.

143

It was time to find a place to live for the winter again. Dad often talked about moving to other places. When things got tough in Eagle, he'd start talking about how we were going to just pick up and leave. With his savings, we could go back to Georgia, but Dad really was done with the South. Not even for another winter. He'd rather go to Holland. Marijuana was legal there, and you could smoke it anywhere.

CHAPTER FIFTEEN

"Maybe Next Year"

WE DIDN'T END up going to Holland. A cabin right out-side the village was empty, so Dad decided he'd look into renting it over the winter. It wasn't wired for electricity and didn't have running water—two major overriding prerequisites.

The cabin had been built by the late Michael David for his family back when he was still young and vibrant with a future that seemed would last forever. It had two bedrooms to the back. The smallest one without any windows was for us girls. We had never had a room all to ourselves, and we loved it even though it was spooky dark. We called it Ryan's Dungeon after the little boy who used it before us. Mom and Dad shared the other room that had more space and a window. The front room was for cooking, eating, cleaning dishes, school, and visiting with company. One corner was put aside for John Charles where he slept and kept his things.

John Charles had earned two and a half thousand dollars by the end of the summer. Dad told him straight up that a grand was going towards rent. If John Charles could earn money like that he could support himself. John Charles was furious about it and resentful. Dad still bossed him around as usual.

As usual, John Charles, Sara, and I took turns cleaning up after meals. "Al, didn't you say that it was against the Bible for a man to do dishes?" John Charles tried to make a stab but didn't get far with his argument.

Dad answered sarcastically, "Yeah, the Bible sez it's a sin for a man to do dishes. Are you a man already?" John Charles wasn't about to keep the debate going. He had long since learned that it in the great majority of cases it would do no good whatsoever.

At least John Charles didn't have to cook. That was one of the chores he could escape. Mom was the only one really good at mending, and since Sara and I weren't as strong as John Charles we didn't do as many of the jobs outside. Our job was to work on keeping the cabin clean. Still it was often cluttered with piles of mess—things that had no home on a shelf or a specific place to rest, unfinished projects, and random stuff that just showed up out of the blue, especially after a mad storm of visitors that lasted all day.

John Charles had his heart set on a good used snowmachine that was up for sell for just $500 so he bought it with part of his summer savings. With a snowmachine, he would be able to go all the way to Eagle to haul water from the wellhouse, run to the grocery store, go pick up the mail during the winter, or visit a friend. Anything to help get away from the house. Even though John Charles had been given the choice to go to public school, he had decided to do home school. He wasn't used to the idea of waiting at a desk for somebody next to him to finish an assignment. He liked to get his schoolwork out of the way and be able to experience life the rest of the time the best he could. As long as he did his chores and lessons, he could explore so many other places on his snowmachine!

In the village, the sky, the river, and the low mountains were bright and open. When a bit of sunshine met with the water of the Yukon, the world suddenly seemed twice as big. The dark of winter did not loom so threatening as when we were living at Gravel Gulch.

Slender grasses that had sprung up during the long days of early summer quickly lost their green and became golden brown, bending in the wind that was bringing winter. Once again, the trees assumed their thin dry skeleton frames, skinny bones that reached upward, suspended with waiting.

Sarah Malcolm lived in the first cabin on the street right on the banks of the Yukon where the official boundaries of Eagle

Village began. She was Gramma Sarah, always sober, constantly busy with beading, sewing, cooking, and looking after children who wandered in and out of her cabin. She still spoke Athabaskan with the other Native elders, and even though her English was broken, she was easy to understand. Her home was just a short walk from where we lived.

Sara and I weren't usually allowed to venture past Gramma Sarah's house by ourselves. After a paycheck from a wildfire, alcohol suddenly flooded the village, and for weeks, almost all of the adults and a handful of teenagers were drunk most of the time.

When too many older people were drunk, the younger kids began to roam around the village looking for attention or food or safety. Some parents became dangerous and went out looking for a fight or adventure in their revelry; others stayed numb and glued to a bed, passed out for days on end during a calm drinking binge.

On many days, children wandered down towards Gramma Sarah's for a bowl of good old-fashioned meat stew. Some became brave enough to come as far as our house hoping Mom might invite them to stay for supper. Mom made all sorts of food that they had never tried before. Black-eyed peas. Cornbread. Dried-apple pie. Leather britches.

Once in a while, Dad would let me walk up to Lena's for a short visit when a drinking binge finally came to an end. Her family had moved from Eagle to the other end of the village. Lena had a special arrangement that allowed her to attend half-days in school while still doing part of her studies at home. Public school, with its heavy duty brain-washing abilities, was still out of the question for me. Since Lena had started school part-time, we no longer did creative writing lessons together. I missed being able to spend those few hours a week with her at Miriam's as we learned new ways of putting words together.

The Natives often had potlatches at Charlie's Hall, the community center in the middle of the village. A little red Episcopalian church stood right beside it, the spiritual gathering building where the Natives met. People often sat on the sturdy benches on the banks of the Yukon, telling stories among one another. On occasion you would see someone sitting alone meditating or working off a hangover as they looked across the vast river at the mountains on the other side. Potlatches were an amazing way to get the community to pull together to enjoy a holiday. And enjoy them we did!

Everyone had something to contribute whether it was helping put out chairs or bringing a special dish. Along with a turkey and all the trimmings, mashed potatoes, and deviled eggs, a table was covered with traditional pumpkin pies, one of Mom's dried apple pies, along with several other desserts. The meal was complete with fry bread perfected by the Natives, a dishpan full of Jell-O mixed with several cans of fruit cocktail, a water bucket full to the brim with Kool-Aid, and hot coffee.

People came to the potlatches dressed to the hilt. They walked to the Hall in warm mukluks that had been carefully handmade and decorated with beaded designs of all kinds. Women wore skirts over jeans, complete with bracelets and earrings, and the more daring ones would bring along a set of high heels for dancing after the meal. Men who had not shown their face for months came along clean-shaven in freshly washed clothes. Even children and babies were decked out in their best outfits.

On Christmas Eve, the gathering at Charlie's Hall was all the more festive. The names of people expected to come were written down on slips of paper about a week before the potlatch. Volunteers worked to randomly give out slips over the next few days, making sure that everyone had a name to exchange a present with at the celebration.

Santa Claus was there to hand out the gifts. Most of the kids wondered about who was trying to fool them. After everyone had opened up their presents, Santa ripped his beard off, still ho-ho-hoing and laughing along with the kids as they talked about which ones had guessed right.

After the gifts and great feast of food and drink, a party began with music kicking in full swing. Tim Malcolm played the fiddle and Howard David strummed the guitar. People of all ages sang along, and as some of the adults drunkenly danced in the middle of the room, the children played with their toys, high on sugar.

Adults often stopped in during the day to enjoy one of Mom's homemade lunches and smoke a joint with Dad. Hopefully, they'd have kids with them, but if it was a school day, I'd be out of luck. The conversation was sometimes a lot of the same. The end of the world. The damned government. The politics of the town. If I wasn't in the mood to do lessons I could just listen to the local news that was broadcast throughout the living room. Forget about Social Studies.

Dad had made friends with a man from Texas who often stopped by to see us. Gene Clowers was in and out of town over the years. When he was in Eagle, our place was always one of his visiting posts. One day, he came in with the latest news that had hit Bush Alaska like a meteorite. According to his report, a creature that looked just like a woman was making its way through villages everywhere. It had hooves for feet and pointy horns underneath its hair. It was epidemic, and there was nothing we could do but hope and pray that we weren't targeted.

Gene hadn't seen the horse-lady himself, but he told us everything he knew. Just last weekend, she had been seen at a dance in Holy Cross, a Native Village more than 1000 miles from Eagle down the Yukon. She could show up at any time, anywhere, completely unsuspected, the devil in disguise.

When I closed my eyes at night, the devil-woman came in and haunted Ryan's Dungeon. Dark shadows crept in and out of the room, and though I could not see them, I could feel them. My heart pounded as my mind raced about trying to figure out what they meant. Was she underneath my bed? How would I know? Why would she be there? Even after I had said my prayers an extra time, sang verses from songs I had learned in Vacation Bible School, and conjured up the sheep to count, I still wondered if I would be her next target.

The story grew the way tall tales do, and by the time I thought I had pushed the beast over a cliff in my mind, Dad said that he saw her walking out of the laundromat. "She had hooves in those boots, and I swear I saw the shape of horns underneath that hair." He didn't have a twinkle in his eyes as he said the words. He just shook his head, adjusted his eyes into focus, and reached for his cup of coffee. "You can't tell me that didn't happen. I saw it with my own eyes."

Other news filtered through the house as the winter progressed. Kenny Drenk had set off with his dog team a couple of weeks earlier, and Helen was thinking the worst. People all over town were beginning to worry. When he finally made it back he was a lot skinnier, two dogs short, and very hungry.

Soon afterwards, Kenny stopped by, dazed and faraway like he had been on a long journey and wasn't quite sure he was back yet. Mom insisted that he stay for dinner before he went back up to Telegraph Hill. He didn't argue the least bit. After he ate everything on his plate, Mama said, "There's plenty, help yourself to seconds."

Kenny didn't need another invitation. He consumed another large portion, licked his lips, and said, "That *sure* beats dog meat."

Maybe evil women with hooves were out there lurking and tromping about in the snow, but Dad didn't let that distract him for long. He had a history to tell, an oral book written in his mind that he told from time to time bringing listeners in with his slow Southern drawl.

If company was around, Dad often got onto a storytelling mode, picking out whatever chapter was on his mind. He liked to talk about how he had married a woman just to have her divorce him and then about how he'd married her again, just to have her divorce again, and then he was on his way to marry her again, but . . . dern it all, Danette couldn't have kids. Deep down, he had high hopes for being a father.

Dad had dreamed about being a musician in Nashville, Tennessee. He had already written a few songs. "I wrote this song for you, Danette. You're probably wondering why I haven't answered yet. You had your chance—in fact you had two. I'm not a' gonna answer 'cause I'm through with you. So keep on a' dialin' till your finger wears off, keep on a' dialin' till your finger wears off, keep on a' dialin' till your finger wears off, I ain't a' gonna answer, I ain't a' gonna talk..."

When Dad had met Mom back in the mid-seventies, he had already changed course. He was a far cry from topping any charts with his country music. His days of Danette were over. He was giving up drugs. Mom threw the biggest fits ever if he drank, so he slowed down on his drinking quite a bit when he met her until it was practically out of the question, but marijuana, tobacco and coffee were a given. "Angel Dust" was just that, left in the dust, and "Orange Sunshine" disappeared over the horizon for good. He was going to invest in a wife and hopefully a couple of strong kids. He ended up with Mom and two little girls, and by then, John Charles had a good set of muscles that just kept getting stronger.

Dad could tell his stories all he wanted and sit around the table passing a joint and smoking a cigarette, but as for me, I had a checkup due every month. I worked on school all morning and for one or two hours after lunch. Mom kept track of the lessons, making sure we were keeping on task enough to get all nine checkups done for us girls to send in by May.

Sara and I hurried to get our daily lessons done as early as we could, hoping to be able to work for only an hour or two after lunch. As soon as we finished, we could work on our other projects, crocheting, beading, or sewing on Mom's little Singer machine that hummed right along until you had to figure out how to change a bobbin.

Mom said John Charles could start public school if he didn't want to do correspondence anymore. But he was fine with his corner as long as he had his snowmobile. He had learned how to do his lessons fast, and he didn't want to sit around in a classroom up at the high school if he could be out riding in the snow.

On Thursday afternoons, Mary Ann McMullin had Bible Club for children at her house in town. John Ostrander, the bus driver, made a special stop to pick up me and Sara when he took the town kids home from school in the village. At four o'clock, the Bible Club kicked off with kids coming from all around. Even Dad didn't mind if we went as long as John Charles picked us up later with his snowmachine.

We sang traditional songs together guided by Mary Ann as she held up signs with the words on them so we could follow along. Mary Ann read us a few good Bible stories and then listened to any of us who wanted to share the verse she had given us the week before to memorize. Every week, I recited my verse perfectly so I could get my sticker for the week. Beside my name on the wall chart, the gold stars stretched continuously.

By spring, I was close to finishing my fifth grade kit. My scores in Math were high enough for me to compete in the cipher-down at the Talent Fair in Tok. Darrel Sonnenberg said I could stay with his family if Dad would let me come in and compete. The Talent Fair was a yearly event where students were given the opportunity to win trophies and ribbons in all sorts of different subjects. The final winners were to be acknowledged at an award dinner and in the "Mukluk News", the local newspaper for Tok.

The bush pilot that would be taking me into Tok was headed out of Eagle early in the morning. He'd be leaving Eagle at five o'clock. Mom woke me up at four so that I had time to get ready. I hadn't slept off all of my supper from the night before. My stomach was queasy. I didn't have an appetite at all, but Mom wanted me to eat a biscuit before I left. "Take another one with you. You'll be hungry for it by the time you get there." I sure was glad for it by the time the plane landed in Tok. Biscuits were always handy at just the right time.

Darrel and Sharon Sonnenberg had a whole tribe of kids. After having kids on their own, they began adopting children into their family. The place was built for a growing family, an ideal home for six or seven kids, along with plenty of room to have an extra kid or two stay for a few nights.

The Sonnenbergs' house was modern with style. It had electricity, hot running water, a microwave, a refrigerator, and a toaster. Everything in the bathroom worked. Even though kids were everywhere, Sharon expected them to behave, finish their homework, and help out around the house. She moved about doing quality control, gently reminding the children to obey the rules, and pick up after themselves.

Tok was a civilized metropolis with over a thousand residents. People rushed about in cars and trucks on smooth paved roads as they headed to work and ran errands. Sharon wanted me to go shopping with her, and she let me push the cart through the aisles as she picked out fresh fruits and vegetables that you'd never see in Eagle.

The cipher-down was the next day. Michael Buck encouraged me to stay calm and clear-headed. "You'll do great. You're the smartest one out there." After I saw the first few students work out their problems, I wasn't as nervous. I knew how to answer ones like that back in the third grade.

When my turn came, the monitor called me up and handed me my first question. I knew the rules. Write the problem down and work it out. You have two minutes. My hands trembled terribly, but I held the chalk tightly in my hand carefully copying the problem onto the board. I then began to think about how to solve it, writing whatever I could on the board that might help me in the end.

Within the first minute, I thought maybe I had it, but then all I could feel were the terrifying numbers behind me—the crowd. More significantly, the seconds were flying by fast, and no matter how fast I tried to catch up with them, I didn't have time to finish the question.

"Sorry, wrong answer," was all I heard as I was shuffled along to make room for the next student. Out on the first round. No second chances.

Before the school year was up, John Charles was able to attend a two-week long workshop in Fairbanks about potential careers in mining. Alaska Gateway School District had offered to sponsor the trip, including the cost of the flight and providing a host family. Dad wasn't going to say no to such a good deal. John Charles had already proven his abilities to earn money if given half a chance. So what if he got to go off to the big city and have a little fun learning how to earn more.

Soon after John Charles returned to Eagle, he said to Mom, "If I get to go again, I want to take aviation. I met some kids that were taking that, and they said that you get to take off, fly around, and land a plane. I sure would like to learn how to do that."

CHAPTER SIXTEEN

"Gramma Sarah"

DAD STILL HAD money left over from helping build the new school in Eagle the summer before. He was able to pay the rent on the cabin for another year, but he wasn't about to have us live in it over the summer if we could be camping somewhere.

By the beginning of June, we were ready to head back out to American Creek Campground in the school bus. Dad found the place to park the bus, and we quickly got to work putting up a makeshift kitchen outside for the summer. While John Charles and Dad put up a tarp to keep it dry, us girls helped Mom organize dishes and food.

I inherited the little green Army tent to have as my own private space during the day, but I still had to stay in the bus at night. John Charles set up the big old blue canvas tent down in a spot closer to the creek so he could have plenty of room to sleep and keep his things.

Before long, we had neighbors. Texas Bob and Sue were back with John Holt in tow once again. Over the next couple of weeks, new travelers arrived, and when they found out they could live for free at the campground, a few of them decided to stay on for the summer. Gold fever spread faster than the common cold in a kindergarten class, and everyone began scrambling to get flakes and nuggets using gold pans, sluice boxes, small dredges, whatever they could afford.

I had long since mastered the art of gold-panning. Dad had taught me to use my spoon to dig deep within the cracks of bedrock, where the gold was most likely to be trapped. I was good enough at gold-panning that I could teach adults how to do it.

All you had to do was tilt and shake the pan with enough force and rhythm to get the black sand and the gold to sink to the bottom. You could go fast at first to get the bigger rocks out of the way, but be extra careful when teasing the last bits of silt and tiny stones away from the black sand. Within and around the sand would hopefully be sparkling treasure: a few grains, the ever-so-fun flakes, a rare little nugget.

Mom, Sara, and I started the summer shift of storing food for the next winter, spending day after day picking wild plants. Our fingers had grown nimble over the years. We worked faster than ever gathering chamomile, rosehips, the new sprouting tips of spruce trees, and Labrador leaves. In the winter, a hot cup of tea was a real treat after working or playing hard outside. If we got sick, chicken noodle soup or Nyquil wasn't on the list for a remedy. Mom believed in the healing power of herbal tea way more than comfort food or store medicine.

John Charles was disappointed that he wasn't able to work at the mine. Harold Nevers was fighting the law and had to shut it down for the summer. The Environmental Protection Agency had accused him of polluting American Creek. They claimed that the number of particles in the water below the mine exceeded the amount allowed by the government. John Charles said, "Last year, there were more particles above the mine than the EPA allows. What are they talking about?"

Harold had to spend months convincing them that he was just stirring up particles. If they were going to be that picky they better figure out how to get rid of some of the particles upstream from the mine or change their standards.

John Charles worked to get any odd job he could in town. He thought eight dollars an hour was a fair wage. That's what Harold had paid him the summer before. Whether he was raking rocks at the mine or painting a relic of a boat for the Eagle Historical Society, he still worked just as hard to earn his cash.

Some jobs didn't pay that much, but Mom said he couldn't work for less than five dollars an hour.

Mom and us girls signed up for babysitting duty so we could earn a little money of our own when the fire crew was out of town. Howard David and Debbie Stevens needed someone to take care of their two-year-old son, Michael. It was a good year for forest fires. He stayed with us so much over that summer that I called him my little Native brother.

Even though Michael couldn't get around too fast, he did his best. As I panned for gold in the creek, he waded in the shallow currents nearby. At night, he slept on a front seat behind the driver's seat underneath his wool blanket. Since he was so little, he had plenty of room.

I needed a curtain so Dad's friends couldn't see me if they were visiting in the bus on rainy days. Mom gave me a good-sized piece of scrap cloth to use. I measured it to make sure it was plenty big enough, sewed a straight hem along the top, pushed a string through it with the help of a big safety pen, and nailed it up on the bottom beam of the top bunk where Sara still slept. I wasn't always in the mood to be in the little green damp tent if I wanted some privacy. My bed was the best place to read on long drizzly days.

I still panned through Texas Bob's tailings every morning, finding more flakes than I could any other way, but I wasn't into bringing him beer anymore. I was tired of being called darling, and I was still finding as much gold in his tailings as ever before.

He sat around panning one evening with a few other miners watching over his shoulders to see if he had hit a vein of gold where he had been dredging the last couple of the days. I sat nearby hoping he'd lose a good nugget as I cleaned raspberries so Mom could make jam. I sorted through them, picking out leaves, little twigs and bugs, and ones that were not yet ripe.

"You got any milk to go with those?" he asked, looking straight at the two little bumps underneath my thin t-shirt. I didn't think Texas Bob was talking about the kind Mom used when she let us make a treat with fresh berries, a little sugar and evaporated milk straight from the can—no water added.

Anybody listening wouldn't have thought a thing about it. Except for me. The question wasn't even worth the barest of an answer. I still gave him a firm reply. "No." Just a bit of small talk as the conversation continued around the tub of murky water.

Before fall began, Dad agreed that we should move back into the cabin on the banks of the Yukon. Grandma and Grandpa and our Uncle Troy had made plans earlier to visit us for a couple of weeks near the end of August. Hosting the three of them would be a lot easier if the bus was right in front of the cabin instead of nine miles out the road.

Grandma and Grandpa got Mom and Dad's room in the house. Uncle Troy stayed in Ryan's Dungeon. The rest of us still spent our nights in the bus, except for John Charles. He had his corner in the front room of the house where he slept.

The mosquito season was nearing the end, and we were having one of the best Indian summers ever. Grandpa wanted to stop and take pictures of wildflowers everywhere we went. He captured the fragile blue forget-me-nots, the pale yellow poppies, and the leftover pink of fireweed that was rapidly going to seed, along with ones that I didn't even know by name.

Grandma wasn't looking down at the ground for pretty colors. She went around complaining instead. "Linda, why on Earth do you want to live up here? I don't know why you had to go and marry Al in the first place. You could be doing so much with your education."

I heard her talking to Mom. "Grandma, where would I be then?"

She stopped ranting and looked over at me. "Well, the good Lord would have taken care of that."

"How?"

"Don't worry your little head about it. That's up for the good Lord to say."

Uncle Troy was a social worker back in Blairsville so he had learned how to get along with all sorts of people. He took most everything in stride, helping to keep an upbeat attitude when things weren't going smoothly. When Sara and I started arguing, Uncle Troy was right there to help stop the squabble. All he had to do was ask a question out of curiosity, and we would scramble to answer him as quick as possible.

157

By the time the two weeks were up, John Charles had made plans to go live with his dad in Georgia to finish high school. Soon after they drove away from Eagle, I felt the chill of a fall wind hit my face. School would be starting soon.

"Mom, you said last year I couldn't go to public school because I already had my boxes." I didn't want to make the same mistake I made last year. "Darrel's not even mailed out the school kits yet. Can I go, please?"

"I'll have to see what Al has to say." I didn't want to hear that answer.

"Mom? Please?"

Dad let Mom know right away what he had to say. "She's not gonna be brainwashed by that system, not if I have anything to do about it. She might as well stop asking if she knows what's good for her." So I stopped asking. For awhile.

Hunting season was in full swing again. Dad had told several people around town about a moose that he had seen a few times down in the valley near Gravel Gulch. Someone soon tracked it down and shot it. They decided to give us half of it since Dad had his eyes on it first.

After that Mom spent day after day processing moose. She cut stew meat and steak to can in jars and ground up chunks for sausage. Sara and I helped by watching the gauge on the pressure cooker and cleaning up dishes. We ate moose steaks, moose stew, moose liver, moose heart, moose tongue, moose sausage, moose meat loaf, moose pizza, moose spaghetti, moose burgers, moose sloppy joes, and little pot pies made out of moose.

Even though we still had to eat moose or fish almost every day, living near the grocery store opened up all sorts of possibilities. If Mom was making homemade pizza for supper, Dad almost always picked up a six-pack of soda pop from the Village Store. He liked his pizza with Pepsi, and he was going to buy it as long as he had any money in his pocket and it was in stock.

Sometimes he brought home all the makings for salad—iceberg lettuce and tomatoes. Sara and I carefully chopped up the tomatoes, but Mom taught us, "Don't ever use a knife to do the lettuce. You have to be gentle with it. Tear it up into little pieces with your hands." As we did the vegetables, she made

Thousand Island dressing with mayonnaise, ketchup, and a dash of Tabasco sauce.

Once in a while Dad brought home a box of ice cream out of the blue. His favorite was butter pecan—if they had it—but Neapolitan was great fun for us all. I loved it when he brought home plain vanilla. We could eat it in the middle of the afternoon, and it didn't matter if it spoiled your supper.

Dad had picked a good place for us to live. We were used to Arlene's by now, with the Village right next by. With John Charles gone, the living room seemed extra big.

The prison of Ryan's Dungeon was the best place in the house though. Sara and I could quietly talk about whatever we wanted without bothering anybody else. I schemed and dreamed of running away. We would leave in the spring before the bears were out. I was obsessed with the idea to the point that I made Sara get rid of her favorite jeans so we wouldn't have too much to carry.

There were a lot of logistics. We certainly couldn't take the Taylor. Dad would be in the van to pick us up before we even made it to American Creek Campground, and we'd get a good whipping just for the walk. I decided we would have to take the Valdez Trail that passed by Gravel Gulch. If a plane happened to fly overhead looking for us, we could hide in the trees. Since the trail hadn't been used for decades it would be overgrown in places, but we'd be able to find our way through where the old path used to be.

I could leave most everything behind—Mom and Dad, the dark, the cold, the mountains and those dreadful schoolbooks—but I had to take Sara. She was coming with me. "We won't need much," I told her. "We can pack some food and wear warm clothes, and I'm taking Sara Elizabeth. And you can take Joyce." Sara loved her little bear that was missing one eye. Joyce had been with her when she was just learning how to talk. "I don't think we'll be ready next spring though. You're still too young. We'll have to wait till I'm fourteen." I said resolutely.

One thing was sure. I didn't have to ask Dad for permission to visit Ricardo Jane Lester. She lived on the other side of the Yukon River in a house with her parents, but I wasn't going to waste any time walking the whole way across when I could just take the train, a grand ride underneath the frozen river.

I sat in Ryan's Dungeon, closed my eyes, and played with Ricardo Jane in her room where her windows welcomed the light and we didn't have to be quiet. Her bed was covered with a clean comforter and plush pillows, all decorated with red hearts and stripes. She had a television on her dresser, but we just played with her toys, spilling them all over the floor for hours before it was time for me to go home. Before I left, I always helped her clean up, putting everything away where it belonged.

Mom was hired as a homemaker taking care of Gramma Sarah. She worked to help Gramma Sarah for a couple of hours every few days. Sara and I could often come along, but we had to finish our morning studies first. We hurried though the lessons because Gramma Sarah had a TV. The box where everything moved around even when it was turned off and everyone was in bed fast asleep.

Eagle and Eagle Village shared one channel—Channel Three. If the TV was on when I went with Mom to Gramma Sarah's, I watched the shows of the afternoon: "General Hospital", "Mr. Rogers", "The Price is Right", and sometimes "Days of Our Lives".

"I got moose stock on stove in kitchen. You take and make a nice soup," Gramma Sarah told Mom, while looking at us girls like we'd better be good so we could watch TV. She continued on with her instructions to Mom, "You get banana chip. Put on plate."

Sara and I would sit very still together crunching away on the sweet dried fruit, knowing not to cause any trouble at all. While we watched the shows, Gramma Sarah taught Mom how to sew tiny beads on moosehide in patterns to make designs of the fleeting pink rose of the spring and the eagle with wings spread against a blue sky. She taught Mom how to make birch bark baskets and mukluks. And she told stories, sharing an Athabaskan word or two along the way. "Mah-see-cho" meant thank you.

When Gramma Sarah started a project with babiche, she wouldn't let Mom use any of it. It was too much too rare. The sturdy strings of pliable hide were tougher than anything you could get in the hardware store by far. Babiche was used to build sturdy snowshoes, strong bags.

Gramma Sarah didn't come off of her own babiche, but she told Mom how to make it. In broken English, she summed up the tasks in simple little steps. "You could do it. Take hide. Scrape all the hair off. Put it in the snow. Scrape it good on both sides. Make it nice and dry. Hold it like this. Cut it like this, like this. Fine, little bit bigger than dental floss. You could make babiche." Her English was easy to understand, but her hands flew in directions that spoke in a way that only those who made babiche could understand. Mom decided not to give it a try.

Sometimes when the TV wasn't on, I couldn't catch up with what happened to my favorite actress in General Hospital or see what price was right at the end. So I sat close by listening to her tell how radio came to the village, and then television, followed by the telephone.

She told me about her mother, Phoebe and of days when people talked in Athabaskan, back when they were a nomadic people. The Athabaskans followed the fish in summer and the caribou in winter. Gramma Sarah was born somewhere in the wilderness on a long walk. "I be dropped on the trail," Gramma Sarah said.

Phoebe pulled everything she needed on a toboggan behind her, and when it came time for Sarah to be born, she left the traveling group and set up a tent of willow pole and hides. After giving birth, with a woman or two nearby, she packed up her little camp, put her brand-new baby in her arms and started walking fast to join the others.

Sara and I could go as far as the graveyard towards Eagle when we were playing outside. That was our boundary. Not far from our cabin, the village cemetery rested in a little clearing between the trees with the road on one side and the Yukon flowing by on the other. We could go to the farthest graves, in the old back rows where cracked crosses had broken under the strength of time and weather, but no further.

I had plenty of time to explore the names. Some had simply disappeared, along with their crosses, leaving nothing but an odd shaped mound behind. Others were barely visible, and among those, Phoebe's name jumped out at me, as faint as it was against the falling cross. I didn't think so much about her bones being right underneath, so close to my feet, but about her name—Phoebe—a bird that flies in the Alaskan sky, a moon circling Saturn.

In one of Eagle's museums, there is a photograph of her with her little Sarah strapped to her back and the Yukon River behind her. Phoebe is a model Athabaskan mother, not smiling for a camera, but keeping a little curve on each side seemingly out of habit. Sarah pokes her head around to see what's happening, and instantly—in one press of a button—one moment is recorded and captured. One culture meeting another for a first time. For all the tourists to see.

One day when the TV was off, Gramma Sarah looked out her window for a long time, somber and thoughtful, out towards the farthest snow covered mountain peak. "See that mountain all covered with snow? I walk all over that mountain. It be on Canada side."

"How old were you then?" Mom asked as they gazed out the window.

"I have two baby."

"What were you doing up there?" It was a long way away.

Gramma Sarah's broken English worked fine for her, and she liked to get straight to the point. "We walk all day. Every day same. We get tired. We walk all day. We walk all day. We trapping. We trap Canada side."

CHAPTER SEVENTEEN

"Never"

IN THE SPRING, Dad announced the news that he was going to buy a house that was up for sale across town. It was a steal at $3,500. He figured that it would cost at least another thousand to have it moved. Dad made a deal that he would put $1,750 down right away and pay the rest when our dividends came in the fall. For the first summer in seven years we weren't going to camp. Dad was ready to settle down somewhere for awhile, and Mom wanted to grow a garden of her own. Sara and I had long since tired of not knowing where we might live next. While there was the mystery that we could eventually live in the equivalent of a mansion (a house with running water), there was also the stark reality that we could end up living somewhere worse than where we were before. That had happened several times in the past.

Dad wanted to put the house on a spot of land in between the graveyard and Arlene's that would give us plenty of room. He made the down payment for the house, and started working on logistics. It wasn't going to be easy taking a two-story A-frame cabin with a steep roof on a five mile trip from the far side of Eagle to the outskirts of the village.

Frank Robbins, the owner of the Village Store, had an old Caterpillar that could still throw some weight around. Dad hired Frank to clear a spot of land large enough for the house, a driveway and a garden. He also paid him to help pull the house down from Eighth Street to its new home on the banks of the Yukon.

A crew helped Dad jack up the house so they could put sturdy logs underneath for skids. The first day they tried to move it, one of the skids broke after just starting off, and so he had to spend a day fixing it. Thankfully, the A-frame hadn't been pulled out to the main road so time didn't pose a problem as far as traffic was concerned, but the next day, a skid broke just before the graveyard on the road to Eagle Village.

They hurried, joining together to jury-rig the remaining solid skids as best as they could to make the trip the rest of the way without the house dragging directly on the ground. By nightfall, it was resting on its new spot of land slightly askew, with the floor still intact.

The last of the schoolwork was almost ready to be sent in, and Sara and I were hurrying to finish. There was way too much else to do. Even though the house only had two rooms—instead of three, like Arlene's—we had the whole upstairs to ourselves. Dad and Mom's bed was downstairs, along with the cookstove, a barrel stove made out of a fifty-five gallon oil drum, a couple of tables, a dresser drawer, and everything needed to make it a home.

The room was 16' by 16' with two big windows and a littler one. Even though the upstairs didn't have straight walls on the two steep sides, it was 16' by 20'. The floor of the extra four feet served as the roof for a good-sized front porch built into the house.

The porch quickly became cluttered with a jumble of things: not-quite broken chainsaws, tools, stove pipe, a battery charger, piles of empty coffee cans for beginning plants early in the house, bags of trash to take to the dump . . . .

A check arrived in the mail from Grandma and Grandpa soon after they had received word of us having a house of our own; $1,000.00 was a long row of zeros, a mathematical incredibility! One thousand dollars written out with Grandma's tidy cursive, with a little 00/100 tacked on at the end.

Soon afterwards, one of the Natives in the village threw a grand moving sale. The spring before, he had brought a new wife up from the Lower 48, along with her children and two U-haul trucks full of household goods. He thought she'd love the place, but his ambitions of building a new cabin for his family in the Interior of Alaska faded over the winter. After the season of renting, his family were ready to be back in the Lower 48, hopefully somewhere a little more civilized and warm.

We ransacked the moving sale, scattering everywhere looking for things we could use. Dad and Mom collected things from all around: a coffee table, four heavy duty folding chairs, a curtain rod with all of its rings, a window shade, a radio, extension cords, tools, paper towels, toilet paper, and a trash can.

Our kitchen would never be the same again. Dad bought a set of stainless steel mixing bowls, pizza pans, a tea kettle, a colander, cookie sheets, a set of mugs, assorted glass plates and bowls, a set of stainless steel silverware, a silverware tray, various utensils, a bread box, Tupperware containers, a set of fine China for twelve, salt and pepper shakers, and the contents of the family's refrigerator.

But the best things of all were two twin-sized beds and two chest of drawers – one of each for me and Sara.

All for $187.

As soon as the weather allowed, Mom planted the garden next to the house. She grew ripe heaps of compost from table scraps, egg shells, rotten fish, and other edible debris, keeping armies of worms busy with their chores. Mom carefully shaped row after row of high mounds of dirt with plenty of room to walk between each one. With the help of water, natural fertilizer, sun, and us, she grew a grand garden. Two greenhouses stood on the edge for plants that needed extra care and attention to thrive.

Sara and I were responsible for filling a fifty-five gallon black plastic barrel with water almost every day from the Yukon. The river was not far from the barrel, but the short hike was steep. It was hard to get up the hill with a five-gallon bucket two-thirds filled with water in each hand.

We both struggled with our loads, tiring and slowing as the water level in the barrel came closer and closer to the top. "Do you think Dad will ever buy one of those water pumps?" I asked, headed up the hill yet again, more than slightly out of breath.

"No," Sara said. "He's got us. Why would he?"

And we weeded, weeds everywhere. A side effect of Mom's green thumb. Once the carrots got big enough to eat, she let us eat a few along the way when we were weeding. And I dared to take as many sweet green peas on the pod as I possibly could without Mom knowing.

Dad got the first trespass notice from the State of Alaska on Sara's birthday in August. It addressed several points with specific details. First of all, our family was living in an area which the State of Alaska defined as the State Buffer Zone of Eagle. It specifically stated that within thirty days, all family members were to be removed, along with any personal possessions, including the house and the garden. Furthermore, we were to leave the premises restored.

It didn't take owning land for Mom and Dad to stand their ground. A week after the road closed, the State of Alaska sent another letter which said that since we had failed to move, they would give us thirty days to write them of our intent.

On Halloween, the warmest one since we had moved to Alaska, the thermometer still read zero degrees. We went trick or treating through the village and didn't even have to wear our snowsuits. The Northern Lights played across the clear night sky while the moon moved slowly overhead. The Yukon was filled with tremendous chunks of ice as it rolled by and continued to freeze.

Just three weeks later, the river ice had stopped running and the temperature began to rest near –30° F. The trespass notices had ceased for the time being. The big shots in Fairbanks weren't so keen on flying in during winter holidays. One morning when it was about –40° F, with the ease of a true weatherwoman, Gramma Sarah told Mom, "Real winter begin now."

It had warmed up by Lena's birthday in late January. Dad said, "You can go to her party, but you ain't gonna stay all night. Her mama can let her have all the slumber parties she wants, but you ain't gonna be staying overnight at no party. You've got till ten. That's it. Don't you even think to ask for eleven. Ten." Ten was late—especially for a birthday party—but, oh how I wanted stay for the part where we slept next to each other in pajamas.

Lena was going to public school, and I was desperate to start more than ever now. Dad continued forward with his mantra of his girls not getting brainwashed by the system by going up to that building where they'll put anything in your head. So I stayed at home, did my lessons with slightly less than half a heart, and read books. The library was always a respite from the rest of it all, a nook in the corner of the world, especially in winter.

I took to tearing out cards from the magazines in the library while I was volunteering. Not all of them. I didn't want the ones that had anything to do with subscribing to a magazine. No, I wanted any that would send me something for free. A catalogue would suit me just fine. So I started getting AARP literature. Sweepstakes invitations. Catalogues from Troy-Built with the latest lawnmower models. Junk mail began pouring in, and John Borg had a talk with Dad about it to see if it could be put to somewhat of an end. I had milk crates full already with what had been delivered to the post office—thanks to all the Business Reply Cards with no postage necessary that I sent away over the months.

Secondhand things were what made our world go round, but I wanted something new. Grandma and Grandpa almost always sent me a ten or a twenty dollar check for my birthday and at Christmas. Every once in awhile when we got a letter from them, they would surprise us with an extra ten out of the blue.

I saved mine to get a stereo. In one of my catalogues, there was exactly what I wanted. It had two tape decks so you could record music from one tape to another. Mom said it was a good brand, and best of all, it was within my price range.

The Fairbanks Mail Order Library had a system down where you could check out up to five tapes for a month at a time. They would pay the postage to send them to you as long as you paid to send them back. And they had a great variety.

I looked over the list of their collection—a dizzying mix of titles that went on for pages. A few jumped out as familiar. Mom and Dad both loved country music, so I knew plenty about Kenny Rogers and Kris Kristofferson from growing up singing songs like "Lucille" and "Bobby McGee".

Oh, and I had developed a close relationship with Def Leppard. I had found "Pyromania" laying on the side of the road a few weeks before I got my stereo in the mail. Even though the tape was cracked and chipped in one of the corners, it played just fine. Sometimes when Mom and Dad were gone doing errands or visiting friends, I'd put it in, crank up the volume, and give myself one of the best headaches ever listening to "rock and roll"!

I had to get Madonna and Michael Jackson. It didn't matter if the end of the Taylor was home. "Like a Virgin" and "Thriller" were required listening all across America, and I already knew I had to get clued in to the news. Now was my chance. But most of the list was a foreign language.

I wanted to learn about the philosophy of the Grateful Dead. Amy Grant—now that sounded like a pretty name to explore. The Talking Heads? Why not? Something unique to bring up in conversation with the village kids.

Darrel Sonnenberg bent the rules for me after I spent some time twisting his arm. I needed batteries—my stereo consumed "D" batteries like they were junk food—and blank tapes. I convinced him that I desperately needed both in order to further my education in music.

My stereo came with the extra perk of a radio, but it was worthless. If you changed the stations, you could get different styles of static, and ever so often a bit of music trickled through the speakers. "What's a radio supposed to do?" Sara asked me after I had fiddled with it one day, hoping to get a faint hint of a human voice.

"If it would pick it up, we could listen to music without even having to put a tape in it. Or listen to news like they do on television." Sometimes it was fun to search through the stations, but I soon grew tired of struggling to find the tiny teases of words in between all the fuzzes.

The upstairs had plenty of room to play and fight, both of which we did to great abandonment. We spread our things all over without worrying about who would trip over them except for ourselves. For the first time in seven years, we hadn't moved to a campsite, and Dad hadn't moved us into the yard. But as soon as the mud dried up a little, Mom was ready to be out of the house so she set up a kitchen in the backyard with a picnic table and a fire pit.

It was a good year for fires so Dad was gone more over the summer than usual. Whenever Dad was out on a fire, the rules changed in our family. Even though Mom struggled sometimes to keep us in line the way he would, she could only be herself in the end. And life was simply different when Dad was gone. With him went so much of the drama, the strictness, the viciousness. But after a very long twenty-one day fire, it was good to see him safely back again with leftover fresh fruit and treats from "Meals Ready to Eat" bags.

With the fire crew back for their few days of "r and r", company was over every day to philosophize, theologize, theorize, rationalize, and so forth. Mom and Dad were excellent hosts; she with her good cooking and humor, and he with his home-grown bud and the way he could tell a story.

Gene Clowers was one of our usual visitors as he happened to be living in Eagle for the summer. He never seemed to change that much over the years. A little older. A little wider around the waist. That was about it.

Except this time, something else was different. Earlier in the spring, I still just thought of him as Gene. Gene Clowers. His still had his usual boisterous way of being when he was talking to Dad, but he had started a habit of staring at me.

The first day I noticed him doing it, he kept his eyes straight on me for a little too long—piercing and gray and intent—before looking away. He did it not once, but twice, and then again. I went upstairs to look in my mirror. Anything in my teeth, a line of ink across my face, an undone zipper? No, none of those. I could not make it out.

Perhaps he was staring at me because I was staring at him. So I went back downstairs and did my best not to look at him. But it didn't take long for me to know that he was staring at me. And I didn't know why.

Dad was called out to fight fire again the next day, and Gene stopped by after the crew had left to make sure Mom didn't need any help with anything. As he left, he finished his conversation with Mom at the front door.

While I waited for him to leave, I leaned against the wall on the other side of the room. The back door was open, sun was shining through the house, and his stares, while not quite as gray, were bothering me again. This time, without warning, he added another piece to the puzzle right as he turned to go. He blew a kiss at me through the air, and then another, like little seeds wanting to land somewhere and grow.

The worst thing of it all was that I wasn't imagining it. And I couldn't tell anyone because they might think I was. Gene had always been so . . . normal. It wasn't like him. But I knew that this was not something that was going to leave my head. The idea had been planted that I needed to keep my eyes open because I didn't want to miss a single clue.

The next day, Mom and Sara went down to the far end of the village to pick raspberries. While they were gone, I heard a familiar motor stop in the driveway. I looked out the window and saw Gene's light blue pickup truck.

The fire crew was still out, and it would have been hard for him to pass Mom and Sara as he drove by on his way into town without seeing them. He had plenty of reason to think that I was home by myself. In that case, I had to get out of the house before he could get in without making it seem like I was overly concerned with him being there. I met him in the yard. I would not act frightened of him. I would make small talk to pass the time. I would see what happened. Directly.

At first he asked where Mom was. "Didn't you see them? She went up the road to pick berries with Sara. She should be back soon. I didn't think they'd be gone this long." I was racing for time with every word, pacing myself as I spoke.

"Yeah, I saw them up there. I was just wondering though— so I stopped by—so, when you gonna give me that welcome home kiss?"

I froze where I was standing, supported by a piece of plywood that was leaning against some trees in the yard. When I started moving again, my whole body was quivering.

My voice was weak and trembling, although I worked to sound as sure and strong as I could. "Never." Then he simply walked towards me, put his chubby palms on my cheeks, and pursed his puffy lips against my forehead. He stepped back from me a bit and looked with that stare.

I looked at him, locked eyes for one last time to help him get the point, and told him, "Mom and Sara are supposed to be back anytime now." Gene didn't seem to be into taking any further chances. He gave me another look and turned around, walking back to his blue pickup truck. As he finally drove away, I went inside the house, thinking things over until I grew tired and angry.

I had to tell Sara. I knew she would keep it a secret. We both knew that trying to get a grownup in trouble could get a kid into a lot more trouble instead. Joining forces with her would help a lot more than letting Mom or Dad know.

Sara listened and brainstormed with me about what to do if he were to make another move. And so when he stopped by a few days later, and said to Mom, "If you need help while Al's gone, put them girls out by the side of the road with the laundry, and I'll take 'em to the laundromat for you." Good thing Mom didn't make us go off with Gene to do errands or insist that we go to church with him when he so nicely offered to take us. She didn't have a clue that he had any motives that were anything but genuine, but she wasn't into making us go into town without her.

After Dad had returned home, Gene passed our house without making an appearance on his first two trips into town. On his third trip in, he decided he had better take his chances. Dad hadn't sent out anyone to kill him yet, but Dad might get suspicious if Gene just disappeared and stopped visiting.

When he sat down with Dad talking like it was old times, I needed to get out of the house. Sara joined me as we finished eating our breakfast. When I wanted another piece of cantaloupe to have with my gravy, she went in and got it for me.

She also took my dirty dishes into the house, and instead of washing the dishes right away, we ran off to play down by the river, skipping rocks and beachcombing until we heard Gene's truck start up and drive away. Then we hurried to do the dishes, so no one would notice too soon.

By fall, Gene was headed back to Texas. A few times before Gene left, Dad took us up the New Village Road to visit him at his house. Lena had moved up New Village Road years earlier. She lived just across the street from Gene's, and I begged Dad to let me go see her, "Please Dad, please? We're hardly ever up this way."

He said curtly, with a hint of disgust, "No, you know you don't need to go over there." Her parents still didn't believe in God, and Dad didn't want me to be exposed to such germs.

So, I sat in the room and looked at the floor, and thought, Gene knows better than to look at me too much now. Gene knew that I might say something about *that* day to Mom or Dad, and if Dad got mad enough, the cops could end up flying in from Tok to see what was the matter.

But I kept my mouth shut. I said nothing to either of them. Sara bided me along. I fought a series of nightmarish dreams, where I defended myself from him, knife in hand. I murdered him finally, in the last of those dreams, blood-red stains everywhere, and death.

CHAPTER EIGHTEEN

"Another Thirty Days"

THE THIRD TRESPASS notice came in the spring, giving my father yet another 30 days to move, but this time with the stipulation that if he didn't, the State of Alaska would take him to court. If Dad wrote a letter of compliance, then they would give us an extra 30 days, two months in all. The letter was due the end of June. Mom responded with what she called a letter of non-compliance. Dad wanted us to stay in our little spot. He was sick of moving. He was stubborn.

Two weeks after Mom sent the letter of non-compliance, the State of Alaska filed a court complaint against Dad. Right away, Mom went to city clerk's office in Eagle to learn about laws that would help her file a response. Even though Dad was the one getting sued, we all had something at stake. Our home. Our garden.

Mom was excellent at research and putting words together using a critical academic style. She typed well and using my old manual typewriter, she was able to make her official documents look quite formal, even if they were presented in an old school sort of way.

Her paperwork was just an addition to the usual responsibilities to preserve food for winter. Berries ripened as the days fell away, the garden grew. The fish swam by. Meals would always have to be put on the table, house or no house, land or no land. And Mom was not only the lawyer. She was also the cook.

According to the paperwork from the court, Dad had to get off state land, along with all said persons. I didn't have to ask Mom what that meant. That just meant us. It didn't matter how old you were, it just mattered that you were a said person. Deadline after deadline, Mom filed her paperwork, always carefully edited and neatly typed. The battle in the court continued over the summer.

Sara and I passed many of our days in the woods next to the house, clearing a little spot of land for a fort. We worked on the ground: pulling trees that were just beginning to grow, weeding bushes that barely reached our waists, and sweeping spruce needles, pine cones and nature's debris in piles to the sides. Trees stood tall above us, sunlight struck down from the sky through their large branches, and every once in a while, a jet flew overhead, grazing the blue with its shocking white contrail left behind.

While Mom researched court rules, statues, and constitutional law to defend Dad's case, he was called on to be the crew boss for a team of wildfire fighters out of Eagle. Eagle had two teams now, so it was especially important for him to be available. For him, it was about earning a living. But for the Bureau of Land Management, it was about having a qualified leader on board. Crews might have to work a full 21 days in a row before being demobilized for three days of rest and relaxation. And after "r and r" they could be sent out again.

When fire season was over, Dad muttered under his breath, "Move? In 30 days? I'm gonna do good to get the heater in and the windows replasticked and this house ready for winter in 30 days. Move? Who do they think they are? I'm moving as fast as I can. I ain't gonna try to move any faster."

I had decided I wasn't going to move any faster with home school. I could care less if I finished the eighth grade. I cheated on my daily lessons. Mom didn't have the time to teach us girls and be a lawyer at the same time. Holding onto the house had become a full time job.

I was sick of home school. Sure, I scored above average in most of my studies as compared to other students across the nation, according to the Iowa Tests of Basic Skills. But I couldn't keep a conversation with somebody my age without laughing uncontrollably over absolutely nothing funny, not even about something that wasn't really funny, but somehow turned out to be funny between two people. No, just nervous laughing—without any control over it. I had to get a grip on how to deal with kids.

When my boxes of books came, I wanted to send them back and go away to a boarding school. There were several in the Lower 48, but they were expensive. Dad made more rules than money, and boarding school was not an option. Besides for the cost, they were much too far away for Dad to keep his keen eye on my behavior.

Most of my lessons were easy enough since the teacher's edition of all of our textbooks were upstairs. All I had to do was cheat. But even cheating could be hard work. Having the answers to the questions helped, but you still had to know how to fill in the missing pieces in between to show that you knew how to do the work.

I absolutely hated my Holt Life Science textbook. Science wasn't a bad subject, but designing experiments and following the rules of the scientific method was a bit extreme. Although it did matter a great deal to me how light affected the rate at which foods spoiled, I wasn't about to try to prove it to anyone. I already knew quite a bit about mold, but whether or not the same types of mold grew on all types of bread was out of my league. And I had already earned the equivalent of an honorary degree in dissection.

If Dad wasn't going to get off of his own high horse about me going to public school, I was quitting. I was not about to start doing lessons at home in high school. They were still free to kids in rural Alaska, but they were based out of the University of Nebraska and structured completely different.

I was determined if Dad decided to keep running the show, he'd have to hold the pencil, or I'd call the law. I might not have the steps down for how to prove a theory, but I knew that you couldn't just drop out of school when you were just fourteen.

Sara was in the fifth grade and needed a teacher, so instead of puzzling over what a frog looked like inside, I took charge of her lessons whenever Mom needed help. Sara didn't care to bother with her Spelling or Math. I had to drag her along in those subjects. I didn't like to draw, but Sara was a natural-born artist, so she didn't need any help there. I wanted to make sure she got her check-ups in on time.

We still had Saturdays and Sundays off from school, and Mom always gave us a good long vacation at Christmas. By the time the holidays came around, Sara and I were free from any pretences at school for two whole weeks. No cheating! No teaching! No worrying about learning!

Dad almost always had something to say about Christmas trees. He'd tell stories about how every time he had cut a tree down for Christmas, they had attacked him in the eyes right afterwards. "Those trees knew what they were a' doin'. You cain't tell me they didn't." And all the while he'd shake his head back and forth as if he would disbelieve it himself if it weren't so derned true.

This Christmas, Dad didn't go on a rant about any trees. He didn't have time to get around to the topic until his fury was already sky high about something else. When we got a package full of presents from Grandma and Grandma, I slipped and lost my footing in my excitement, falling right on top of the typewriter. I heard a loud crack right away.

Dad lit into me like a match dropped into a forest that hadn't been rained on in a month. My throat churned as it tightened, and as I struggled to keep my breath steady, my eyes started to water slightly. I bit the inside of my lower lip to distract myself so I wouldn't cry.

Mom moved slowly towards the typewriter, her features strained as she took the piece of the carriage return from my hand. "I can still use the other side. I'll just have to return it myself. It'll just take a little longer." She turned the knob of the left side several times just to make sure. Each click moved an imaginary line up an invisible page of paper.

Right after Christmas, the temperature dropped, staying between $-30°$ and $-60°$ F. The water and laundromat in the village froze up, and the generator in Eagle quit running. Then the back-up generator stopped working right after it was started.

Even though Eagle and Eagle Village were without electricity, telephone, and television, time kept on ticking. At least everyone could still get water at the wellhouse in town. Governor Cooper declared a state of emergency, and help quickly arrived to help fix the generators.

Our family wasn't all that affected with no electric power to lose, no phone to stop ringing, no pipes to freeze, no television to update us on the news. The oil heater kept our house warm, and Sara and I continued to work on our lessons, homebound with our books and school supplies.

As the winter progressed, Mom worried about the river thawing in the spring. If the ice backed up, a flood could take our house away before the State of Alaska would have a chance to plow it to the ground.

She asked the chief of Eagle Village, "Is it safe to live so close to the river as we do?"

He said in broken English, "No need to think of that now. Think about that in May. River not going to break today."

Gramma Sarah lived even closer to the river than us. She always wanted to be ready if a flood happened. She told Mom, "Every spring, I pack up little clothes, little food, just in case we have to go."

When we heard the first crack of the river ice, it was as if someone had fired several shotguns at the same time. We stood in the yard, waiting to see what would happen. Over the next several hours, the ice began to push north ever so slowly at first, stopping and starting again and again as the current of water rushed underneath. For days, the ice kept grinding forward leaving behind massive blocks of ice—as big as houses or cars—on the banks of the Yukon.

The struggle in the courts intensified as summer neared. New dates were set for the impending eviction. The latest paperwork said we were to be off the property, with any and all portable possessions by May 15. The house was to be removed from the grounds by June 20; otherwise it would be destroyed on June 22. Mom and Dad stood their ground.

The State of Alaska wavered when it came time for demolition day. Instead of bulldozing the building down in a mad frenzy just to have it gone, they decided to put it up for sale, with minimum bids starting at $100.

After just a few bids John Borg's father-in-law bought it for $300. He was an older man who was only in town for a short while. He didn't own any land in Eagle, but John and Betty Borg's place would be a fine place to put it for a time. Anything to keep it from being pushed into the river. I spent the afternoon in a wretched mood, walking on the beach of the Yukon without even the heart to look for a pretty rock.

Without the A-frame, we went back to living on Telegraph Hill. Sara and I slept on the old bunk beds that Dad had built for us, and Mom and Dad had their bed to the back of the bus. The area was cluttered and crowded, and by late August the temperatures were beginning to drop significantly, especially at night. The frost got the garden, which the State hadn't been concerned with auctioning away, and we spent an afternoon in half-frozen dirt digging potatoes alongside of where our house had been, leaving a mess of jumbled roots and disturbed ground. The few leaves left on the birches were a stark yellow, and a wind whistled through our campsite with a tune that could only mean winter was coming soon.

CHAPTER NINETEEN

"The Next Door Neighbor"

"MY DAUGHTERS AIN'T gonna be in that system. I'm not allowin' it." I had started to tune Dad out when he'd start into that mantra. I didn't want to hear anymore about how I wasn't going to public school. I was done. I wouldn't do home school anymore. Dad could beat me till I was dead, and I wouldn't care. I'd call the law and tell them that I was only fourteen, and that Dad wouldn't let me go to public school and because I had dropped out of home school, he was breaking the law. Maybe then, Dad would go to jail. If he did manage to keep me on correspondence, he was going to have to hold the pencil for me. I was done writing to his tune.

Mom was about as done with home school as I was. She wanted to keep teaching Sara, but if I wanted to go to public school, she wasn't going to stop me. Still Dad was the one in charge, and he had decided long ago that his girls weren't going to get vaccinated. That was the one thing I had to factor in the equation. The law was on his side there. You had to have your shots to get into school; otherwise, you might get another kid sick.

My stubborn side kicked in to the max, and I sent a letter to a church in Fairbanks asking what I had to do to become a Christian Scientist. If I was a Christian Scientist, I could get a religious exemption. They responded with a very polite letter saying that I was welcome to come to church for the services to learn more about Christian Science.

I couldn't take a quick trip into Fairbanks for a special initiation session, and I didn't see what use letter-writing was going to get me. Especially since I didn't want to be a Christian Scientist at all. I just wanted to get into Eagle Community School.

It was starting to look desperate. I was about ready to let Dad go into me worse than he had before and advertise it to the whole town if I wasn't able to go to school. And he was not about to break down and let me get a single needle in my arm. Not over his dead body. Mom took me down to the school when it was time to register so that we could have an emergency visit with Mary Morris, the secretary of the school. Ms. Morris was always great at knowing what to do. After fumbling through a few stacks of paperwork, she found a form for Mom. "Just fill it out, and add that you need a religious exemption there on the bottom." When Mom was done, the secretary signed it in her italic way, mary morris, with two little m's. She was just that way. She never bothered to capitalize her name even if it was against the rule.

Dad was checkmated. Of course, he was going to sue somebody. There was always somebody he was going to sue. But Mom had already been a lawyer for one of his cases, and she wasn't looking for the job again.

Every morning, I set my alarm, waking up before anyone else in the bus. I didn't bother with building a fire to make hot oatmeal. There were almost always leftover biscuits in the breadbox. After one or two of those covered with peanut butter and some thick homemade jam, my fingers were freezing in the morning chill of the fall air, and I was ready to get on my second-hand Schwinn ten-speed to fly down the hill to the public school.

Even though we were considered dirt poor in Eagle—thanks to Dad's belief system—I worked hard to fool the kids at school. Grandma and Grandpa always kept track of my measurements and told me to send in pictures of things I liked from catalogues to help them while they were shopping. So I had frosted denim jeans and new brand-name tennis shoes with stripes just the color I wanted, along with the best of all—a frosted denim jacket.

If I thought I looked okay on the outside, it helped me feel okay on the inside. Even though new clothes helped me feel pretty, I was seriously afflicted with acne, and no stylish outfit could undo it. Sometimes it faded away for a short while, but then a terrible outbreak would hit again. Then I bit at my nails and chewed on my cuticles in futile attempts to keep from bothering my zits. It was a never ending battle.

The ride down the hill was getting chillier every day, and September turned into October. Dad had found a place to rent that was in a sweet little corner not too far away from the library. The cabin was built to suit a real family, with three rooms in all. Monte Worner was leaving for the winter, along with his wife and a toddler and a new set of twins. He wanted to rent his cabin to one of his friends, and Dad was the perfect fit. It had three rooms in all—a little bedroom to the front of the room for Mom and Dad and a big loft enclosed upstairs for us girls. Thing is was our winter was coming faster than Monte's was starting.

We started moving in while they finished packing. Mom and Dad still stayed in the bus on the hill, but Sara and I started sleeping in the loft that would soon become our bedroom. After a few days, Monte and his family were gone, and the place was all ours, complete with a sturdy outhouse.

The cabin came with electricity. Dad decided he would keep it on for the lights, but the television and the microwave left behind were put in a closet that was padlocked for the winter. They were not to be a part of our home. Nor was the telephone. Dad had it unhooked right away. People could stop by if they had something to say, or wait.

Dad wasn't completely unreasonable about the electricity. I could use it with my stereo and the new alarm clock I had just bought at the hardware store. He even let me put my old butane powered curling iron in storage and use an electric one instead.

The wellhouse was just a walk away. The kitchen area off to the back of the house had two sinks, plenty of counter space, cupboards, and drawers. Cleaning up after meals was easier than ever. And the laundromat had since moved to town.

Eagle Community School was tucked away in the trees about five blocks from Monte's. But when the temperature was –55° F—not counting the wind chill factor—the idea of blocks faded away as a familiar chant began in my mind. "I'll get there soon . . . , I'll get there soon." It was worth the walk just to get out of the house, even if it would be easier to go backwards, depending on which way the wind was blowing.

The schoolwork was easy, but I hated P.E. Wasn't walking to school and back in arctic winter conditions enough physical education? We were supposed to wear shorts and t-shirts during P.E. So I went out and bought a razor and started shaving my legs when I took showers at school. Any little thing to help myself fit in with the crowd.

As for any after school activities, I could forget about them. Dad won that hand. That meant not being on the basketball team. Everything in P.E. was about basketball. Every year, the basketball team got to go on a trip so that they could compete with Dot Lake and Chistochina, two villages right outside of Tok on the Glenn Highway.

I didn't want to learn how to play the game. I felt in the way. So the principal said I could run or walk around the gym instead. Sixteen times around made a mile. I ran, until I ran away from the rest of the room. The solitude of the space in the lines outside the playing field became my own ground until the class ended. Maybe the ball would fly out of bounds, but someone was almost always right by to keep it from getting in my way. In the off chance that it was coming straight for me, I struggled to catch it and toss it back without it hitting the floor.

The school was still almost brand-new. The gym was fully enclosed in the building, along with bathrooms with showers and lockers. Kids who were in kindergarten on up to the third grade shared a common classroom. Another classroom was set aside for students in middle school, along with a separate room used for Math and Science for the kids in middle school and high school.

Terry McMullin, the principal of the school, had his office area set up in the main classroom used for high school students.

Computers lined the wall, complete with Mavis Beacon typing lessons and the game called "The Oregon Trail". A lab to one side of the room gave us plenty of space and everything we needed to do our science experiments.

Mr. McMullin didn't let you slide in class, but he wasn't all about scribbling about things that happened ages ago on an eraser board. He did plenty of that, but once in awhile, he would let us have a party. While we made popcorn in the school kitchen, Mr. McMullin would set up the school TV and the VCR and let us watch a movie just for fun. The kitchen was equipped to host dinners for the entire community on special occasions, but it wasn't used for the students during the week. The school didn't have a lunch program, so all the kids had to bring theirs from home.

I loved homework. Homework didn't mean nine boxes of books that had to be done by May. It meant something short to do at home to turn in the next day. It further distracted me from my inalienable surroundings.

There were only about ten of us in high school. Joel and Katrina were about to graduate, but there were four eighth grade boys who would be graduating from middle school and moving on up into high school. For now, all four freshmen were girls.

There also happened to be three young men in Eagle who were all twenty-eight years old and single. One of them had moved into town in November, ready to start out a winter. From the very beginning, I was curious as to why Phil chose Eagle, especially at that time of year. But more than that, I wanted to know what was behind those blue eyes of his. I wanted to feel him close to me for hours on end. I thought about him, about when he visited . . . .

He stopped by the house even more often as he got to know Mom and Dad. I watched him during many of his visits, paying attention to what he had to say to them or to anyone else who happened to be over at the same time. I recorded serious mental notes of *any* conversation that happened between the two of us for later reference.

The best vantage point was often from the small vent upstairs that helped circulate the air through the house. It was like a little window that looked down on the living room. I couldn't see the blue of his eyes from that far away, but I could memorize his face and listen to him speak with his slight drawl and soft voice. He had such a smile. I had fallen in love.

When Phil told me he liked the music by Amy Grant that I played upstairs, I recorded him a mixed tape of her songs that I thought he would like the best. The next time he was invited to stay for dinner, I ever so casually gave it to him. "You said you liked her. I have another one of these, so you can have this one."

Before he even had time to say thank you, I looked at him like he couldn't say no. I was all ready to insist that I didn't need *two* of them. "You do? I'd love it. I'll listen to it at home. Thank you."

"You're welcome. I have more by her if you want to borrow any." Gospel music was innocent enough when it came to making friends with adults who came by to visit Mom and Dad, especially the ones that were like big brothers and sisters to me.

Dad was presently more concerned about me getting pregnant if I spent thirty minutes doing anything with one of the high school guys outside of school hours. And there was the all too real chance that I could end up being a pagan by default of spending too much time at Lena's.

When I learned that Phil went to the library on Friday evenings, I began to volunteer for the shift. He liked to sit in the little rare book room that was tucked away in an open corner behind the barrel stove and look at magazines. When he returned books on my shift, I took them home to learn a little more about what was going on in his mind. I liked that Phil had picked the best astronomy book in the adult section. By perusing his book selection on the sly, I learned little clues to help me talk with him a little when he was visiting. I wanted to be prepared every time he came to visit to have a little connection with him outside of anyone else. Music. A comment about a constellation or a reference to a complicated mathematical equation. Anything for me to have between just the two of us before he walked out the door.

When spring came, he just up and left. I had no idea how to get in touch with him. I missed seeing him terribly. I listened for news, but nothing. A few weeks later, my family was visiting Greg and Audrey and their little girl, Amy. Phil had been renting a cabin from Greg and Audrey over the winter. As we were getting ready to leave, I noticed an address for Phil posted on the wall among other slips of paper. I recorded it in my memory, my mind filled with hope that I might meet with him another day. At least for now, I could send him a letter to tell him how I'd felt all along. Supposedly, he was in Fairbanks.

I used my best cursive, writing down what I had wanted to say, things that just couldn't be said when he came over to enjoy one of Mom's suppers or smoke a joint with Dad. Things that I wanted to say when we were by ourselves in the library on Friday nights, but didn't have the courage or the knowledge as to where to begin. How much I loved the gentle gaze of his blue, blue eyes.

But I did not dare mail it. I tried. I had the letter all ready, addressed and stamped and ready to go. I walked to the post office. I looked at the drop box for the mail, and while my heart was screaming, "Drop it in! Drop it in!" I would not do it. I lingered to dream of it for a little while—to think about what mystery would emerge from me being so bold. And then I walked away, letter in hand. I simply could not send it. The mystery was just too big.

As soon as summer arrived, Monte was back in town, and our lease was up so we would have to move. Dad decided we would camp out at the bottom of Telegraph Hill in a clearing set right back from the Taylor where others had camped in years past. So far the State wasn't doing anything about anyone living in the City Buffer Zone if the home was on wheels and ready to drive away at a given moment. So we headed back up to camp in the bus at the bottom of Telegraph Hill in a clearing set right back from the Taylor, and Sara and I traded in the grand upstairs of Monte's for the old set of bunk beds we had once so much loved.

Before too long, Phil was back in town. It didn't look as if Fairbanks had done him any good. He came to see us up on Telegraph Hill once in awhile, and was very distant at first. But after a few visits, he was Phil as I remembered him before—oh, the sparkle in those infinitely prismatic blue eyes! I was glad I had not sent my letter. It would have perhaps destroyed the mystery.

The bus was a great place to live compared to a tent till August, or even a week or so afterwards, but by the beginning of October, it started to feel like a jail. And a very cold jail at that. Dad knew it all too well from the year before. By the end of August, he had already rented our next new home.

Darrel Sonnenberg owned a cabin just outside of town on the far end of Front Street that Dad could rent year-round. It had a loft, a separate bedroom, an L-shaped room for everything else, and electricity. Dad had decided we could continue to keep the electric. He was going to take advantage of it to grow marijuana indoors over the winter where it could thrive with proper cycles of light and a nonstop fire burning in the barrel stove.

Dad, Mom, and a healthy set of baby plants got the main bedroom to the back of the house. Sara had the loft to herself, and the smallest half of the big L-shape was just for me to use. A good curtain would help with privacy—and unlike a wall—I could keep it open whenever I wanted. During much of the day, my room was in view. I wanted company to admire my poster of Johnny Depp. But most of all—I wanted Phil to visit—so he could see my little niche in the house. I always kept my curtain open for him.

Sara had started public school. She was in the seventh grade. Since we now lived on the other side of town, we were on the bus route, and the driver was good at keeping to his schedule. But even if he was late, waiting in the cold for a few extra minutes was way better than having to walk several blocks on days when it was −50° F or −60° F.

The high school had two seniors, no juniors, four sophomore girls, and four new freshmen boys. I was one of the sophomore girls. On the average, fifteen-year-old girls are more mature than fourteen-year-old boys in many ways. It didn't take long for a couple of them to prove it to us. One afternoon, a high school girl was taking a shower in our locker room, and when she heard the muffled laughter right next to her, she began to look around and saw several holes that went all the way through the wall. Somebody was watching her—

looking directly at her—and it seemed like it was likely more than one person.

She quickly got dressed and went to report the incident to the principal right away. He soon learned that a couple of the freshmen boys had been going to the boiler room via the school attic. They had figured out where the wall of the girls' shower room was in relation to the boiler room, and after a little work with a hand drill they had full access to live soft-core porn. Us.

Terry McMullin disciplined them by putting them in separate carrels in our classroom for three days, but we had our own punishment to dish out to the boys. The silent treatment for a month. Unless it interfered with our grades, we wouldn't talk with either of them about anything.

One of the seniors started to show an interest in me. Secretly, I still had my eyes on Phil, but he was much too old, and I was too shy. Jeff was handsome enough, athletic, smart, and tender, and much closer to my age. We held hands. He bought me a ring in the shape of a heart, and then— my first kiss! But something was missing.

I was madly in love with Phil. At first, I thought he might disappear like he had before, but when he started renting a cabin across the street from Greg and Audrey, he suddenly became our closest neighbor. The options seemed endless. I daydreamed about all the ways I could get to know him better.

Phil began to stop by to see us most days. At first, I began to trade a few tapes with him, talking a little about music whenever he visited. While he was watching me practice chess one day with my computerized board, I learned that he knew how to play the game a little. So I challenged him. I carefully set up the pieces, making sure that the queen was on the right color, and began to think about how many different moves could possibly be made between the two of us on the board.

After that, we began to play chess regularly. We took our time, contemplating our moves with great care. Dad sat unknowingly by as I looked into the mirror of Phil's soul. I saw so much of myself there, and before long my brown eyes—the color of rich soil—caught Phil's attention for good.

Mom noticed, but she didn't talk about it with Dad. My friendship with Phil was something she would not destroy.

When I went for a walk, he oftentimes surreptitiously joined me along the way, and we played in the woods like little children, building little rooms on the ground from sticks and twigs. He gave me flowers and passionate kisses. We talked about the little world we had created together—rich with life, music, chess, literature, nature, and love.

Dad was too busy keeping his tabs on the high school boys to even notice. One night when he was out playing poker with his friends, Mom said that it would be okay if one of the freshmen came over to our cabin so I could help him with his homework. When Dad got home later that evening, I heard him ask Mom if anybody had stopped by while he was gone. Phil sometimes came over on poker nights to visit with Mom and play a game or two of chess with me for something to do, and Dad never seemed to care. Some people, like Phil, had just become part of our family over the years. But the freshmen guys were not included in that group, and Dad wanted to make sure that everyone knew it. Even though the holes in the girls' bathroom had long been pasted over, Dad had not forgotten about them.

Mom mentioned that Junior Brinkman had been by for a couple of hours to work on a school project. We had studied at the kitchen table in full view of Mom, but that didn't stop Dad from being plenty mad about it though. The first thing the next morning, he lit into me. "What were you doing having that boy over here last night? Studyin'? You might fool your mom, but you can't fool me. I know what y'all are up to, and I ain't havin' it in my house."

As the months passed, Dad made sure that I knew he was still the boss. My incriminations were turning into all out wars between the two of us. When he decided I needed to be put in my place with a stick or his belt, I tore out my hair and banged my fists on nearby furniture. It was one of the best ways to end a fight. The basic rule was that I won if Dad stopped before I did.

After a particularly rough episode one day, Dad was most certainly the winner. I had pulled hair out to no avail, and several of my knuckles were already bleeding from hitting the counter. Still he was crazy with anger. He grabbed me by the hair, and as quick as that, he knocked my face against the kitchen table and broke a plate.

The next day one of our friends came to visit. They did a double-take when they saw the deep gash on my chin. I could do some serious surgery on my acne, but this was no cystic zit gone wrong. I just glared at Dad. There—I thought to myself—you be that way, and everyone will see.

Soon afterwards, John Charles would visit us before he headed back South. Then the two paths of my destiny ultimately diverged—one leading to the prospect of marriage to the man I loved most and the other to those bright lights of the big cities. So on that grey Saturday in early August, I chose to leave it all behind—the Dad, Mom, Sara, the town, the village, the kids, and Phil.

Epilogue

ON ONE OF my trips up to see Dad, a funeral was being held for a beloved old-timer of Eagle Village. The procession took us around the loop of the village—everyone driving slowly with great respect—and then on up to the graveyard. The following day, I went to the memorial service with Dad at the little red Episcopalian church right next to Charlie's Hall. Several people were drunk and others quite sober—each crying or laughing or being silent in their own unique way of longing for a dear spirit who had just left them.

The crowd opened the hymnals to "Amazing Grace", and I listened as Dad sang along with his deep Southern drawl of a voice. As I joined in, I stopped thinking about the Daddy I once knew. Instead I remembered the old man sitting next to me—*my father*—who was simply singing a song about grace and it being amazing.

I managed not to cry until I drove out almost two weeks later. I was listening to a mixed tape of several versions of "I'll Fly Away" and then Emmylou Harris started singing "Precious Memories" . . . and oh, how they do linger. I had already finished the Taylor Highway and was driving deeper into the south of Alaska. The leaves were still on the trees—green with just a faint hint of gold beginning. I cried for miles then—with sun sparkling over the mountains—snow just starting to cover their pointy caps.

Few people know the beauty or the curse of that land where I was first exposed to the wild and wonder of Alaska. A peaceful kind of lonesome pain lies deep within me when I recall the days and years I spent growing up there. I do not abandon my nostalgia. Instead I keep this corner of my country close to my being. No matter where I now journey, I always carry with me these memories of my Alaska, of that place where her woods provided my family a shelter from the rest of the world, her mountain walls standing tall around us, her sky a ceiling above us with the circling sun of summer, the waxing and waning of the white winter moon, the stretching reach of sweeping stars, and the glorious stream of the northern lights that sometimes danced across with their greens and yellows and pinks.

Now on clear days in the summer when I am back in Eagle for a visit, I like to take a quiet run, with the sun on my skin and the sky blue overhead, ravens flying above and beyond me, my feet traveling over the dusty roads of my childhood. I run much the way the Yukon River runs, calm and sure on the surface, wild and angry underneath, strong and persistent.

CPSIA information can be obtained
at www.ICGtesting.com
Printed in the USA
FFHW022355181118
49485014-53845FF

9 781457 507649